Thought is Free

Ouyang Yu came to Australia in mid-April 1991 and has since published 146 books of poetry, fiction, non-fiction, literary translation and criticism in English and Chinese languages, including his award-winning novels, *The Eastern Slope Chronicle* (2002) and *The English Class* (2010), his collections of poetry, *Songs of the Last Chinese Poet* (1997) and *Terminally Poetic* (2020), which won the Judith Wright Calanthe Award for a Poetry Book in the 2021 Queensland Literary Awards, his book website www.huangzhouren.com and his bilingual blog youyang2.blogspot.com

He was shortlisted for the Writer's Prize in the 2021 Melbourne Prize for Literature and won a Fellowship from the Australia Council in late 2021 for writing a documentary novel. His sixth novel, *All the Rivers Ran South*, is coming out in mid-2023 with Puncher & Wattmann and his first collection of short stories, *The White Cockatoo Flowers*, is forthcoming in 2024 with Transit Lounge Publishing.

Also by Ouyang Yu

The White Cockatoo Flowers, Transit Lounge Publishing, forthcoming 2024
The Sun at Eight or Nine, Puncher & Wattmann, forthcoming mid-2024
All the Rivers Ran South, Puncher & Wattmann, forthcoming late 2023
Foreign Matter and Other Poems, Ginninderra Press, 2022
Terminally Poetic, Ginninderra Press, 2020
Living After Death, MPU, 2020
Small Says: Words, Stories and Mini-meditations, also as No. 35, *Otherland Literary Journal*, a single-copy edition, Otherland Publishing, 2020
Spring Waters: Li Yu, the Emperor of Poetry, also as No. 32, *Otherland Literary Journal*, a single-copy edition, Otherland Publishing, 2020
West of the River, also as No. 31, *Otherland Literary Journal*, a single-copy edition, Otherland Publishing, 2020
Flag of Permanent Defeat, Puncher & Wattmann, 2019
Billy Sing, Transit Lounge Publishing, 2017
Fainting with Freedom, Five Islands Press, 2015
Diary of a Naked Official, Transit Lounge Publishing, 2014
Bilingual Love: Poems from 1975 to 2008, Picaro Press, 2012
The Kingsbury Tales: A Complete Collection, Otherland Publishing, 2012
Triptych Poets: Stuart Cooke, Bronwen Manger, Ouyang Yu, Blemish Books, 2011
White and Yu, PressPress, 2010
The English Class, Transit Lounge Publishing, 2010
Loose: a wild history, Wakefield Press, 2011
Chinese in Australian Fiction: 1888–1988, Cambria Press, USA, 2008
Reality Dreams, Picaro Press, Sydney, Australia, 2008
The Kingsbury Tales, Brandl & Schlesinger, 2008
On the Smell of an Oily Rag: speaking English, thinking Chinese and living Australian, Wakefield Press, 2008
Bias: Offensively Chinese/Australian, Otherland Publishing, 2007
Listening To, Vagabond Press, 2006
Moon over Melbourne and Other Poems, Shearsman Books, UK, 2005
New and Selected Poems, Salt Publishing, 2004
Foreign Matter, Otherland Publishing, 2003
Two Hearts, Two Tongues and Rain-coloured Eyes, Wild Peony Press, 2002
The Eastern Slope Chronicle, Brandl and Schlesinger, 2002
Representations of Australia and Australians in China and Hong Kong: 1985–1995, Centre for the Study of Australian Asian Relations, Griffith University, 1998
Songs of the Last Chinese Poet, Wild Peony Press, 1999
Moon over Melbourne and Other Poems, Papyrus Publishing, 1995

Ouyang Yu

Thought is Free[1]

Acknowledgements

'Thought is Free', *Meanjin*, Vol. 81, Issue No. 3, Spring 2022, pp. 56–64
'This essay is 7368 words', *Overland*, issue 246, Autumn 2022, pp. 33–57
'…billions of deteriorated or rebellious cells…', *Against Disappearance: Essays on Memory*, eds Leah Jing McIntosh and Adolfo Aranjuez, Pantera Press, 2022, pp. 227–238

Thought is Free
ISBN 978 1 76109 562 7
Copyright © text Ouyang Yu 2023
Cover image: Ouyang Yu

First published 2023 by
GINNINDERRA PRESS
PO Box 3461 Port Adelaide 5015
www.ginninderrapress.com.au

Who cares tomorrow about an idea we had entertained the day before? – After any night, we are no longer the same, and we cheat when we play out the farce of continuity. – The fragment, no doubt a disappointing genre, but the only honest one.

Emile Cioran, *Drawn and Quartered*, p. 166

子曰：'予欲无言。'

A man should learn to detect and watch that gleam of light which flashes across his mind from within, more than the lustre of the firmament of bards and sages. Yet he dismisses without notice his thought, because it is his. In every work of genius we recognise our own rejected thoughts; they come back to us with a certain alienated majesty. Great works of art have no more affecting lesson for us than this.

Ralph Waldo Emerson, *Selected Essays, Lectures and Poems* (pp. 150–151)

(The author-editor's note: when one reaches sixty-five, one realises one's life is nearly at an end, all the more reason to read and write, to read-write. Words are but a trigger of memory at every turn. Autobiography is biography one writes of one's own dead self. Non-fiction is but fiction without pre-designed chapter headings. It's a flow of words, mixed with memories, smells of thought from day to day, poetry breathed in and out, and, ultimately, things experienced by someone living as if exiled out of this world, 'separated from the separated'[2] in a nearly posthumous existence. I shall not go beyond 50,000 words for each book of this, as I promised to David, so I'll conclude the thing today – O.Y., 10/7/2021)

♪♪

I came across a remark by E.M. Cioran, who said,

> To deprecate your own kind, to vilify and pulverize them, to attack their foundations, to undermine your very basis, to destroy your point of departure, to punish your origins…, to curse all those non-elect, lesser breeds, torn between imposture and elegy, whose sole mission is not to have one…[3]

And I was reminded of *Songs of the Last Chinese Poet* (1997), in which I wrote, in Canto 2,

> thinking of destroying everything
> thinking of destroying a civilisation
> a civilization as long as the footwrappings of a feet-bound woman
> we are a dying race
> no longer can we live on our own
> but must we metamorphose by losing our tongue
> our beautiful sexy body
> into something we would have been ashamed to see
> something hairy something so self-centred
> that only a TV set can match.

I'm growing to like Evelyn Conlon's *Skin of Dreams*, and I underlined a remark by Maud in the book that goes, 'We're supposed to say yes these days, yes to everything. To say no is a perversity.'[4]

Not long after, when I drove to Bundoora to post a few books to China, I handwrote a poem that I transcribed in word that goes,

What I wrote while driving to Bundoora on Plenty Road

> the sky over here
>   is called
> indifference
>   every day
>   is a
>   no

    that's 365
        nos
        for you
    multiplied
        by 30
    who wants to
        no this?
    who cares?
        who gives a
        fake?

(Copied at 5.45 p.m., Friday 5/3/2021, at home in K, based on a handwritten one done in my car at 3.51 p.m., in Plenty Road on my way to Bundoora Post Office.)

Checked into FB. Saw a famous writer's news about his new book. Only one 'Like'. I clicked 'Like' as a thought came to me: no amount of big awards won can guarantee people will like you forever.

    A couple of hours after, when I went to the loo, this expression came to me: 文人相轻: literary beings belittle each other.

    One can write a whole book about that topic but the core of the truth remains: there is little mutual regard between men and women of letters or characters. FB is such a superficial place one just has to stop bothering about it.

2002, I think it was, when I went to San Francisco to attend an international conference on Chinese diasporic writings, I went on an outing with Hong Ying, a bus tour. My memory is fading. But I remember the moment the thought came to me because I paused and said to her, by the window, 'I've found the solution.' She was bewildered and I explained that this was to do with my novel in progress. I didn't give her any more details. But, as soon as I returned to Melbourne, I gave the story a new twist in that one of my characters in the Burma Road left the army and became a wartime tourist, roaming the mountains in Yunnan.

My thought sequence should actually have been reversed because I thought of that after I had read this, again by Cioran, who says,

> Faced with the Nile and the Pyramids, Flaubert thought of nothing but Normandy, according to one witness – nothing but the landscapes and manners of the future Madame Bovary. Nothing but that seemed to exist for him. To imagine is to limit oneself, to exclude: without an excessive capacity for rejection, no plan, no work, no way of realizing anything.[5]

The novel I wrote then is *The English Class* (2010).

Before my collection of prose poetry, Living After Death, was launched by him, Kevin Brophy had a chat with me over the phone to check a few things. Among other things, I asked him not to use the tired adage, 'the angry Chinese poet', because it's not me as there are other qualities such as humour and love.

Yesterday when I picked up *Joseph Roth: A Life in Letter*s, I came across 'a sort of poetic spleen'[6] and I thought, Oh, yes. That's perhaps what I have to do from time to time and everyone has to do, from time to time, too. Why the label, and such an unfair one, too?

When I came across this remark by E.M. Cioran that goes, 'Man makes history; in its turn history unmakes man',[7] I was sharply reminded of Nicolae Ceauşescu and Muammar Muhammad Abu Minyar al-Gaddafi, with their violent deaths, achieving a perfect balance in their lives of rise and fall.

In the Second World War, John Curtin was known to have said that he 'wanted to hold this country, and keep it as a citadel for the British-speaking race…'[8]

I have always thought that what I'm speaking apart from Mandarin Chinese is English until I came across that, feeling that if I had known it was that, I would not have decided to learn the language in the first place.

It was only yesterday that the thought came to me while I was having a walk outside in the park that the last straw on us is the arrival of fully robotic beings to replace us. What do we do if that happens? Lie in state alive?

Then this, again from Cioran, 'Everything indicates that humanity is going downhill…'⁹

It's more downhell, in my opinion.

E.M. Cioran and Cao Xueqin. How different are they? Perhaps as different as Rumania from China or Australia?

But when Cioran said that 'Harmony, universal or otherwise, has never existed and never will exist',[10] it sounds close to what Cao said in a poem in *The Dream of Red Mansions* that I'll approximate in my translation below,

Everyone knows that gods are good
But no one can forgo achievements and fame
Where are the ancient generals and ministers?
All gone, leaving behind a grassy mound

Everyone knows that gods are good
But no one can forgo silver and gold
They complain that they never stay together long enough
But when it is long enough their eyes are closed for good

Everyone knows that gods are good
But no one can forgo his beautiful wife
When you are alive, she makes you feel good
But when you die, she goes with someone else

Everyone knows that gods are good
But no one can forgo his own kids and grandkids
There are so many loving parents since ancient times
But filial kids and grandkids are very few

If things are like that, where can one find harmony? Perhaps, the only harmony one can find is harmoney, a word I wilfully coined.

I think I've entered into a state of posthumousness. I don't know what happened before I was born till years after I was born. I shall never know what will happen when I die. Now that I think I am already dead and I am living a dead man's life, in a country that is most suited for that purpose, I am literally futureless. Being futureless, in other words, is being deathful. Or being alive. Then it's fitting to quote Cioran again, near the end of his book, where he says,

> No more past, no more future; the centuries collapse, matter abdicates, the shadows are exhausted; death turns to ridicule, and ridiculous too is life itself.[11]

As I said in a poem I did this morning while having a walk outside in the park, in this country everyone dies-lives, their hearts pieces of ice.

In Martin Heidegger's *Being and Time*, 'It has been maintained that "Being" is the "most universal" concept.'[12] I just had to laugh at it for being so preposterous. For one thing, 'being' as a word is untranslatable into Chinese. For another, the closest thing it rhymes with in Chinese is 病 (bing), a disease or condition.

That something so serious as 'being' is dissolved in ridiculousness in another cultural and linguistic context serves as a reminder that unless the universe in that 'universal' contains the rest of the universe it is not a complete one.

'...the villages themselves – they want to be cities.'[13]

This remark, by Joseph Roth, in his novel, or novella, *The Emperor's Tomb*, that I came across this morning, standing pissing in my loo, caused me to award it with an underline, with my red pen.

I recall a visit we, poets from Songjiang, made to the village where a postgraduate student of mine's home was based. It's not a village. It's a town with tall buildings and wide streets, accessible by car. The only difference is that the village-city borders on the rice paddies and a hill not far away where there are orange trees for profit. The village has an enticing name: Houma, literally, Back Horse. Or Rear Horse, if you like.

My village, the one I was sent down to for re-education in the early 1970s, had a path leading between two ponds across a creek, with forty households in a row, from east to west, or from north to south, overlooking the ponds. That's how it still remains in my memory. I have never been back since.

Then, this, where Roth says, 'My hearing is acute, so I pretend to be a little deaf,' (p. 2) which won another award of a red underline from me. Please note that I have read so many books without even bothering underlining a single line. But this, in a matter of two pages.

Because it reminds me of this landlord's son in *my* village, who had a habit of not hearing anything unpleasant chucked his way although he was known to have acute hearing. In those days, if you had a landlord for a father, you were like a Jew in Nazi Germany. Or you were like a Chinese in Australia in the gold-digging days.

I grew increasingly interested as I read the account of John Sampson's story, who 'was active in a dispute with the mine-owners and formed the Australian Miners' Union,' and 'was promptly dismissed and was never employed in a mine again'.[14]

Why was I interested in this? Because it coincides with an Australian organisation that I have worked for over two decades not giving me any more work for no reasons at all, very recently, at about the time when I read this. And I was not even in dispute with them; I had only sent queries.

Working as a contractor, one is not in any way protected by anything. And that's Australia for you, formerly known as 'the Workingman's Paradise'. Go and keep cheating the migrants with that.

♪♪

Goethe is a practitioner of self-censorship. I worked this out from reading his poetry in Chinese, translated by Qian Chunqi. The poem in question is 《你为何赋予我们慧眼》 (roughly, 'Why did you bless us with intelligent eyes?'),[15] with a footnote to the effect that Goethe wrote the poem about Charlotte von Stein, claiming that she and he were husband and wife in a previous life. But he did not include the poem in his collected works.

I was interested in this because I have now entered into a period of massive self-censorship. One word that is typical of my life at this particular stage is 'cut'. Cut, cut, cut. Cut, cut, cut. It's the singing of a bird called Self-censorship. One cuts oneself dead even before one dies. The more so in an age of utter political correctness. How can one even breathe, being so squeezed by correctness? Does one stop shitting altogether because shit is bad and it pollutes the environment?

Although Kazuo Ishiguru, oops, Ishiguro, warned the young writers against 'self-censorship', it's easier said than done. He doesn't have to because he believes he is in 'a privileged and relatively protected position' (https://www.bbc.com/news/entertainment-arts-56208347). What nonsense! Is he a God already?

♪♪

Breakfast. A conversation between the husband and the wife.

H: Just came across the Queen's 'Never complain, never explain' rule. (See here: https://www.smh.com.au/world/europe/how-meghan-blew-up-the-queen-s-never-complain-never-explain-rule-20210309-p5798k.html)

W: I heard you. I understand.

H: It's always about being positive. When I was a teenager, Mother got very worried when she heard me sigh a sigh. She said, in her Wuhan accent, 'But a boy like you shouldn't sigh. A young person should never sigh.'

W: Yeh, you do like complaining.

H: So do you, so do all the Chinese people.

W: Australians do that all the time. In the shop I ran, Australian customers complained all the time. That's what they like doing the most. That's also why people don't like hiring them because they complain so much, never happy with anything.

Hours after, when I tried to find the same article, I found something different, with an additional message, that goes, 'Never Complain. Never Explain. Never Apologize!' (https://www.nytimes.com/1970/05/10/archives/never-complain-never-explain-never-apologize. html)

And I thought, how similar that last line is to the Chinese Communist Party claim about itself being always great, glorious and correct? Only when you are always correct, you will never apologise.

Two artists met at lunch, one female and the other, male. The female is a sculptor. The male is a thoughter, one who has thoughts.

Immediately, he delivers his first thought to the sculptor, while eating. In the next art show, divide the gallery into prison cells, complete with everything, from CCTV to the toilet, with a full-body scanner at the entrance and an X-ray system. Those who want to physically experience what it is like to be in a prison can pay for entrance at a fixed price. Special sessions are preserved for company CEOs at a much higher price because they are the ones who can pay and their costs may even be tax-deductible. Overnight accommodation in the cells may also have an appeal to those with weirder tastes. The title for the exhibition, tentatively, is 'In Prison, with Maximum Security, the Australian Way'.

Without waiting for her to make a comment, the thoughter plunged into his second thought, which is a project called 'Doing Ju 死 tice', a bilingual wordplay on 'Doing Justice', with 's' replaced by the Chinese word for death (死). The idea is simple enough: Hire someone to kill someone.

To be more specific, the idea is to pay someone innocent to kill someone guilty, so guilty that he has killed more than thirty or fifty people in one go, like Port Arthur or Christchurch, but manages to survive the mass murder unscathed.

'Then see if he is subject to capital punishment?' said the sculptor, amazed.

Ignoring her and plunging into his third thought, the guy merely found the link and sent it to her by WeChat, saying, 'Check it out. It's my idea in a nutshell: http://cordite.org.au/poetry/domestic-enemy/invading-australia-a-sequence/'

Perhaps I should have corrected myself by referring to him as the ideas man? For the moment, though, I like the incorrectness of the new coinage, 'thoughter'. If you say 'I thought', then that 'thought' is a verb. See what I mean?

♪♪♪

Kenneth Koch, whose exuberance I love, has a line in his poem 'The First Step' that goes, 'Nothing but Chinese absence soup'.[16]

My immediate reaction to this is, 'There is no such soup', followed by a wonderment if that is a soup in which nothing Australian exists.

Still, I like the soup and what diverse images it helps evoke.

♪♪♪

I often wonder if our solitude – I mean my own solitude – is not a direct result of the total extermination of insects around me, such as flies, mosquitoes and tiny little insects, crawling or flying. When we are as clean as the detergent itself – when I, I mean – what hope is there for a living being alive with other living beings in a shared community of lives instead of a detergent living being alive till it is dead and purified in the fire, or purifired in the incinerator?

This is the thought that came to me as I took my morning walk in the nearby park, bathed in the morning sun and accompanied by no one, not even a fly, only singing birds in the far trees, as well as something I had read last night in bed. When I got home, I found the passage that goes, recording what an Aboriginal leader by the name of Regal Black Swan said to an American woman,

> Everything in Oneness has a purpose. There are no freaks, misfits, or accidents. There are only things that humans do not understand.

You believe the bush flies to be bad, to be hell, and so for you they are, but it is only because you are minus the necessary understanding and wisdom. In truth, they are necessary and beneficial creatures. They crawl down our ears and clean out the wax and sand that we get from sleeping each night. Do you see we have perfect hearing? Yes, they climb up our nose and clean it out too.[17]

Then he added,

Humans cannot exist if everything that is unpleasant is eliminated instead of understood. When the flies come, we surrender. (p. 69)

Curiously, a rhyming couplet we were taught as a child in China came back that goes,

Zhuangjia yizhi hua, quan kao fen dangjia (庄稼一枝花，全靠粪当家). [Good crap, good crop.]

Since when did they start replacing human excrement with chemical fertilisers? But if Australia is a country without philosophy, as someone from Europe claimed years ago, to the indignation of some intellectuals here, the Aboriginal remark above is philosophy enough, good for the human crop, too. The human brain crop. We don't have much of it here, do we?

Last night, I thought of something and put it down in two fragments: 'characterless tombstone' and her wish to 'remain unknown'.

Now, night again and time to expand on them. Wu Zetian (624–705), China's first and only woman emperor, had a tombstone erected in her honour that had no inscriptions on it. Hence its name 'wu zi bei' [Characterless Tombstone], a tombstone with no inscriptions as she ordered, 'character' referring to the Chinese characters as compared with the English words.

I had intermittently wondered about the mystery of this and of Chinese women in general until last night when, perhaps for the hundredth time, I recalled again this woman's wish to remain unknown, not only for the rest of her life but also for the rest of her death, not wanting to keep any traces of her life on record or even wanting to be written about.

I know her. But I can't disclose any details about her except that there is a strong connection, I feel, between the woman emperor and her, a woman commoner, for reasons that are beyond me.

To be honest, I found it quite touching, in a mysterious way.

I went to the city to have that lunch by tram yesterday. Someone sat down next to me and started talking, to himself mainly. Everyone else looked the other way. I kept reading, lending one ear to what he was talking. It was all gibberish until a young woman sat down opposite him when he started talking to her as if they had known each other for a long time. I heard him say to her, 'Were you born in Australia?' The answer was yes. Then he said, 'You look very young, only fourteen.' The answer was no, and wavering, hesitant, embarrassed. The man carried on for the entire length of the journey till the woman left. Then he stood up and went to the door, preparing to disembark. Then he changed his mind and went to another door as a string of expletives rolled off his tongue. People stared. I, about to disembark, stared, too. He didn't seem unhappy. He just talked and kept saying 'fuck you', his eyes raised skywards. No one knew what he was talking about or with whom he was angry.

Just now, in one of my numerous visits to the loo, I picked up Cioran's *The Trouble with Being Born* and read,

> 'Life seems good only to the madman,' observed Hegesias, a Cyrenaic philosopher, some twenty-three centuries ago. These are almost the only words of his we have… Of all oeuvres to reinvent, his comes first on my list.[18]

'I must go and check him out,' I heard myself say to myself, finding the coincidence so felicitous and thinking, perhaps we don't need philosophers in Australia as long as we've got them elsewhere.

♪♪♪

I took a photograph of the books I read per day – thirty-two in total – and added a caption, 'These are the books I read on a daily basis.' Before I posted both on Instagram, I had changed my mind and ditched the idea, part of the cancel culture for you, with a question, to myself: why bother? Whose likes do I want? Then I started reading one of the books and found this that I underlined and copied:

> In 1983 she [Helen Quach] became ill. Needing medical attention and total rest, she came back to Sydney and bought a house overlooking Sailor's Bay. Apart from treatment and rest, she also spent her time reading and studying operas, only occasionally conducting concerts. Although she had received a Western education, Quach inherited an interest in Chinese culture and thought. In recent years she has shown a tendency towards introspection, as evidenced by her study of the philosophy of Laozi and Zhuangzi, and her time spent in meditation.[19]

I continued to read, and to copy, what Leonard Bernstein had to say about her:

> Miss Quach runs the danger of being a pretty young woman, and thus conquering all hearts for non-musical reasons. But her performance as our assistant this season (1967–68) has given us reason to believe that she will succeed on musical grounds as well. Her rhythmic sense is sharp, her reflexes are quick, her address to the orchestra captivating. She seems to be at her best in works of large dimension (odd for so diminutive a creature), and if there is such a thing as a Maestra, Miss Quach could well be it.[20]

I hate to explain myself. But if I have to, I like the reference to her inherited interest, something that is ever so slightly slighted in this country.

♪♪♪

Ralph Waldo Emerson says, 'To believe your own thought, to believe that what is true for you in your private heart is true for all men.'[21]

'Is that right?' I said to RWE. No response came. All 'men' or 'all women'? My question continued. 'What if I say I like social media less and less and I hate clicking the "Like" button more and more? Would you have any clues?' I said to RWE. Again no reply.

Out on my daily walk, I recently had a thought visiting me that human beings are ants that have to keep moving around and doing things or else they get rusty and die, which reminds me of a poem I wrote years ago by the window of an airplane I was sitting in, to the effect that however great and important you are, no one can see you from up on high. So what is the importance of self-importance?

Then this, from Cioran, that I read, following that random thought,

> To think is to undermine – to undermine oneself. Action involves fewer risks, for it fills the interval between things and ourselves, whereas reflection dangerously widens it.
>
> ... So long as I give myself up to physical exercise, manual labor, I am happy, fulfilled; once I stop, I am seized by dizziness, and I can think of nothing but giving up for good.

Two unrelated incidents, in one of which Liu Shaoqi (1898–1969), former vice-president of China, persecuted to death by Mao, once said that workers preferred to be exploited by the capitalists as they couldn't live without being exploited, and in the other of which a postgraduate student of mine failed multiple examinations until she found a job, perhaps a permanent one, only to find that it's taken all her time, including weekends, from nine a.m. to seven p.m. every day.

Can anyone stop me from including these seemingly unrelated matters?

As soon as I saw a sign of protest on Instagram this morning, saying 'DON'T F*UCKING TOUCH ME', held by a woman protester, my mind was immediately taken back to Confucius (551 BC–471 BC), who said, 'Nan nü shou shou bu qin (when a man and a woman give or take something, they mustn't touch hands)'.

He said that about 2,500 years ago. What has changed?

♪♪

When I won awards, I gave a speech off the cuff. In 2004, when I was awarded the Innovation Award in the Adelaide Festival Awards for Literature, I said, from memory, 'This book [*The Eastern Slope Chronicle*] had been rejected twenty-eight times across the world before it was accepted for publication by a publisher that had first rejected it…'

Then, in 2011, when it was announced in the awarding night that my novel *The English Class* had won the Community Relations Award in the 2011 NSW Premier's Literature Awards, I, slightly tipsy, stumbled onto the stage and delivered a speech off the top of my head, part of which ran thus, from memory: 'I don't remember how many rejections I received before this book was published. But it seems to me that one is pressed down and further down until one cannot go down any further. That is when one rebounds and rises to the top,' or something like that.

I recalled all this when I read the following by Cioran that goes,

> At the lowest point of ourselves, when we touch bottom and *feel* the abyss, we are suddenly raised up – defense-reaction or absurd pride – by the sense of being *superior* to God. The grandiose and impure aspect of the temptation to be done with it all.[23]

♪♪

Alongside cancel culture is the culture of praise. Who doesn't want to be liked, and praised? People, whether you are colourless or of colour, all want that, even people in the past, for example, in *Romance of the Three Kingdoms*, a fourteenth-century Chinese novel. Before the kingdom of Shu Han falls, its king Liu Shan leads an immoral and dissolute life, paying no attention to the impending threat from the kingdom of Cao Wei, and putting all his trust in a sorceress who, after a performance of seeking God's advice, informs that the Kingdom will triumph over the enemy come what may,[24] an ancient example of how praises can lead to complacency and defeat.

Now that books seem to be written for the sole purpose of pleasing, praising and winning awards, or losing them, I am constantly reminded of how the book I am reading came about, with its author who 'dared not publish it in his lifetime' because of his attack on the hypocrisy of the Victorian era. (See here: https://en.wikipedia.org/wiki/The_Way_of_All_Flesh)

The book in question is *The Way of All Flesh*. Does anyone dare not publish his or her work in his or her lifetime now? Is there any point of doing that any more?

I like what Mencius (372 BC–289 BC) says about the eyes when he said,

存乎人者，莫良于眸子。眸子不能掩其恶。胸中正，则眸子瞭焉；胸中不正，则眸子眊焉。听其言也，观其眸子，人焉廋哉？

And here I render an instantaneous translation:

Nothing of a person that is both inside and outside him is more expressive than his eyes. If one's heart is in the right place, his eyes are bright. If not, they are dim. When you listen to him talking and observing his eyes, where can he hide his good and evil?

I thought of the shifty eyes. That's what I thought.

After I finished reading *Sanguo yanyi* (*Romance of the Three Kingdoms*), I went out for a walk when a poem came to me and I dictated it to my mobile phone as it turned the speech into words, as follows:

Can they really correct anything by being correct?
Can they really correct anyone by being correct?
Can they redeem themselves by being correct?
Can they erase memory of violence and death by being correct?
Can they vaccinate themselves by being correct?
Can they institutionalize themselves by being correct?
Can they insure themselves against future accusations of them
                              criminally correct by being correct?

Towards the end of the novel, Sun Hao, the last emperor of the Eastern Wu, is known to have picked up a habit of getting all his ministers drunk in night after night of drinking parties, only to get his guards to check who behaves himself badly and to either remove his facial skin or gouge his eyes instantly if he is caught in the act of wrong-doing, a political correctness par excellence, putting any current varieties to shame.[25]

In Mao's time, if someone recited Mao's sayings wrongly, he or she would be kicked out of the school or lose his or her job. And, to cap it all, one wouldn't begin one's day without quoting something from the Little Red Book to match. The only thing that comes close to it is the current trend in the acknowledgements of country in Australia.

I have been increasingly feeling so cowed and choked by something I can't put a name to in this country that I find it more and more difficult to speak my mind about a lot of things any longer till today when I came across this by Cioran, who said,

> We come closer and closer to the Unbreathable. When we have reached it, that will be the great Day. Alas, we are only on the eve…[26]

Exactly. I know what it is, and I know you know I know you know, too.

In *Australian Nicknames*, by Taffy Davies, I came across 'Cecil X' as a 'workmate with a Polish surname, hard to say and harder to spell' (p. 31, Rigby Ltd, 1977) and thought, 'How true!' as I recalled a novel by Alex Miller with a title that I could never say or spell. I'll Google it. Right, it's (let me just copy it) *Prochownik's Dream*.

I suspect in knowing that and doing that, the author was deliberate; he wanted to challenge how far the Australian version of multiculturalism could go and how knowledgeable it wanted to be about others and their names. He's certainly not trying to make it easier for his readers.

Then, last night, I met Cioran, in his book, who said,

Never try to make things easier for the reader. He will not thank you for your trouble. It is not understanding that he likes – he likes to mark time, to get stuck, he likes to be punished. Whence the prestige of certain murky authors; whence the perennial appeal of the hodgepodge.²⁷

There you go. But I like that challenge and I, too, like to make challenges from time to time, a typical example being my *Flag of Permanent Defeat*, which I doubt if 0.01% of Australians can understand and even want to read.

♪♪♪

It's Quach again. But I think the following is worth quoting in its entirety:

In her youth, Quach was known as the 'female tyrant of the podium' – she was used to shouting and stamping her feet at her musicians when she was not getting the required effect. Her interpreter would always turn her most dramatic demands into gentle entreaties. Consequently she dismissed her interpreter and conducted in English.²⁸

Why did I do that? Because the American interpreter, in interpreting the talk between China and America, allegedly added fuel to the fire by doing the job the hard way, thus incurring anger on both sides. See this Chinese article here: https://mp.weixin.qq.com/s/ZE_AC5wDXxxA- fcpa5X5cQ, its Chinese title meaning exactly that, *Adding Fuel to the Fire: The American Interpreter Magnified Blinken's Offensiveness* (火上浇油！美方的翻译，放大了布林肯的攻击性).

Today is Saturday 20 March 2021.

♪♪♪

The man sat in bed and raised the book high as he said, 'This is the book! The best of all books. It beats the daylights out of all, or almost all Australian books.' The woman said, 'What's the book? The man said, '《大卸八块》.'

When they lay down, side by side, the man started telling her about the author. 'He was born and bred in Romania. At twenty-one or twenty-three, he published *On the Heights of Despair,* a truly original book. Then he went to France and lived there till his death. But he wrote in French and it's said that his French is as good as that of the best French writers or even better. He's a philosopher, but a poet-like one because he wrote bits and pieces, fragments, each like a pearl with thought shining through it. He dares speak his mind because he was beyond prizes and awards as he rejected all the prizes that went his way. The worst thing about the present-day culture of ours is its push for recognition by way of prizes and awards. So much that has won them is not worth reading and is forgotten when the author is dead.'

Why bother who this man and this woman are as long as we know that such a story has happened and has become part of the Story?

By now, the novel I have written over the last couple of years has gone through fourteen drafts, although I still think the first draft is probably the best and a friend of mine I showed it to said to me after he read it that he was very 'moved'. But the more I revised, the more I felt it was contrived, cleansed and sanitised, becoming more and more readable, acceptable and marketable, more shitty.

Cioran approved it, long ago, except I only got to know it yesterday, when he said,

> Perhaps we should only publish our first drafts, before we ourselves know what we are trying to say.[29]

Years ago, before I even read a single word by Cioran, I had said I was against revision, particularly the Australian kind of revision. I said that rather than keep changing positions in lovemaking, one would be far better off to take it right to the end.

I have an example of anti-revisionism in a poem in my *Terminally Poetic* (2020)

This poem has been revised at least three times

I was writing this poem I mean I was writing this poem in english
no I mean I was writing this poem in English
about the possibility of revision but I wasn't able to write it
and I ended up with something that I wasn't able to revise
no I was saying that I ended up with something that I was not able
to revise no I mean I was not able to write something better
than what I had intended to
but actually I did intend to write something that I was not going
    to revise
I mean I did intend to write something in its first draft
no actually it is better to revise and have multiple drafts
because it conforms
and confirms our view that writing is a mechanical process
I mean a mechanical process my spelling is poor
I beg your pardon our culture is superior because it is revised to
    whiteness
by deleting all the unwanted colours
yellow contains a low
black contains a lack
I am only repeating myself from a novel I wrote a few years ago
that remains unpublished
'cause it needs revision as a white woman suggests
a white woman is so beautiful so white so revised
I want to fall in love with her or in Chinese climb up love with her
oh white woman you don't find me containing a low and a lack
because I can't revise?
but I'm telling ya I have revised this one for at least three times

I bought this book for two bucks. But I did not put down the date when or the place where I bought it although, at the bottom right corner of the first page, I wrote, '2020.5.4 夜开读于家中厕边.'

    On p. 200, I wrote, '从此不再细看了。2021.2.15 黄昏时于厕上．'

    Then, on the last page, I wrote, '2021.3.20 下午4点多从 Hanging Rock 回来后小便时速看毕!'[30]

I didn't feel guilty. I felt even less so when I read this by Cioran that goes,

Only unfinished – because unfinishable – works prompt us to speculate about the essence of art. (*Drawn and Quartered*, p. 65)

The only thing that interested me is the size of short chapters, sometimes only one-page long, the rest ignorable.

Su Shi, also known as Eastern Slope Su, has one line in a poem that goes, '雨脚半收檐断线'[31] (the foot of rain is half withdrawn as its line is broken from the eaves).

I love the image of 'the foot of rain' (雨脚), an expression I learnt as a child but have managed to completely forget in Australia till a couple of days ago when I read it in a book I bought twenty-two years ago in Huangzhou, where he was sent into political exile for five years, producing a wealth of prose and poems, including some of his best, somewhat similar to my voluntary exile in Melbourne, where I have lived for thirty years, producing some of my best writings in prose and poetry and in both English and Chinese, too.

Castration of books, a thought. In China, they castrate pigs and that makes the pork very eatable. In Australia, they don't castrate them and that leaves the pork smelly and hard to eat.

When it comes to books, they castrate them in China. Unlike the castrated pigs, the castrated books are not very good to eat (read). In Australia, they also castrate the books. But they nicely refer to it as editing. The edited ones are never as good as the first drafts, I think.

Reading Emerson, as quoted before, actually, still the Foreword, where it is said,

Emerson is the spokesperson for the idea that the poet is a sayer more than a maker.³²

Well, depends how much technology was available to E in his days although I agree, in spirit. I, for one, say poetry on a daily basis in my daily walks in the local park except yesterday. I got my iPhone 10. I speak into it as I walk. My voice is instantly turned into English words or Chinese characters. With a minimal amount of editing, I have a poem created. As soon as I start my walk outside, poetry comes to me and is achieved that way.

But, yesterday morning, I told myself to stop. And I did. Still, in Notes, there are more than seventy poems waiting to be copied and recorded in my computer, such exhausting labour.

Want to know how the highest art is formed? Read this quoted passage:

Emerson stands for the idea that the highest art shapes its own form, unique and organic, from within, as a pear grows.³³

Now, that's exactly how this book is being formed, taking no cue from anyone and going its own way.

I'm reading *The Gulag Archipelago* by Alexander Solzhenitsyn, a book I had for years, possibly over twenty-five, shelved away. Ten pages into it, over a space of twenty-six days, I found it tedious, too much about how terrifying arrests were. By comparison, China's achievement in completely reforming the mind of its intellectuals during the Cultural Revolution was much more terrifying because they were turned into automatons without a word of protest or faced the fate of Zhang Zhixin, whose throat was slit as a result of her open opposition to the Party.

Martin Heidegger talks about 'Being', as being 'of all concepts the one that is self-evident,'³⁴ but that sounds to me like an imposition. 'Self-evident' to whom? To Germans? English? French? And all the rest of them whose language is letter-based, with 'is' and 'are' that can be turned into 'being'? What about the Chinese language, in which there is no 'is' and no 'are' and even the closest equivalent 'shi' (是) does not change with time, remaining 'shi', singular or plural, in all times, not translatable as 'being', a word not translatable into any appropriate Chinese word, either?

What preposterousness in assuming that that is 'self-evident'!

At one stage, Liu Xiaobo allegedly said that it would be best to get a foreigner to run China and when a white Australian friend of mine heard that he responded that to run Chinese affairs would tire him out, whoever it was.

In reading Freud's *Totem and Taboo*, I was amused to learn that, in numerous societies, to occupy the top position of a country is to have one bound by numerous taboos to the degree that many would try to run away. In one instance, 'most tribes were obliged to choose foreigners as their kings',[35] in Sierra Leone, for example.

To be frank, my naivete made it possible for me to agree with Liu around the time of 1989 and think that the Chinese people simply could not manage their own affairs properly and had to be somehow managed by a foreigner by invitation.

When the people of a country wholeheartedly embrace that idea, colonialism is at its most successful.

If this sounds like a diary or journal entry, let it be. I said four poems in my phone this morning in my walk along the Fairway via Tee Street through Bundoora Park. Two English, two Chinese. I didn't plunge into poetry straight away. I walked. I photographed. I walked again. Then, a poem came. Let me copy it here. If it's not good enough, let it be. You are not the judge. No judgements are welcome here.

Blame the sky blame the people blame the rest of the world blame oneself Blame that country blame this country Blame the rain blame the sun Blame the birds blame the weeds Blame the cold blame the heat Blame the impossibilities blame the choices Blame the virus blame the foods Blame that country blame this

I made a couple of changes on the way and just now. Then, near home, another poem came, and I record it here, not for you – I don't have a reader – but for myself,

I don't want to know I don't want to buy I don't want to get in touch I don't want to call back I don't want to go I don't want to come I don't want to read a single line I don't want to click likes I don't want to look I don't want to see I don't want to bother I don't want to say hi I don't want to have anything to do, Not them, not us

Enough said. Time for a shit, for a second time. (I shall provide a self-edited version of the two poems if in the right mood.)

I feel like quoting something. I feel like doing it now. Here you go:

No one can know about the level of my agitation – constant and powerful – about everything under the sun. I am never at ease.

It felt like this was me talking when I read it. Then this:

Tell me why a great writer isn't duty bound to accuse his country instead of praising it.

That's exactly what I thought. Did Joseph Roth know that as a migrant writer my writings wouldn't be deemed publishable if they contained country accusations?

Both quoted from his *A Life in Letters* (p. 49).

I'll found (a verb) a poem shortly, from someone quoted before, one of them anyway. Done, as follows (it took less than 3 minutes, said to make you feel jealous, there being so much jealousy around these days),

Rehearsing

I was in perfect health I felt better than ever
Suddenly I was cold

so cold that I was sure there was no cure for it
What was happening for me?

Yet this was not the first time I had been in the grip of such a sensation
But in the past I had endured it without trying to understand

This time I wanted to know and now...
I abandoned one hypothesis after the next:

it could not be sickness; not the shadow of a symptom to cling to
What was I to do? I was baffled

incapable of finding even the trace
of an explanation, when an idea occurred to me –

and this was a real relief –
that what I was feeling was merely a version

of the great, final cold –
that it was simply death exercising, rehearsing...

(11.04am, Monday 22/3/2021, at home in K, a found poem from E.M. Cioran's book, *The Trouble with Being Born*, p. 194)

He says,

> A book should open old wounds, even inflict new ones. A book should be a danger. (*Drawn and Quartered*, p. 67)

Can't agree with it more, knowing perfectly well I'm in Australia, a country down under that needs constant praise from people that it wants to put down under.

♪♪

When Cioran says, 'I have known no one who loved failure so much; and yet she killed herself to escape it' (*Drawn and Quartered*, p. 66), I thought of putting it away in a folder for future quotation purposes because I was composing my next novel about a woman intellectual based on one of my aunts.

Can't tell you more than that.

♪♪

Mencius says, *You buyu zhi yu, you qiuquan zhi hui*. That's more than 2,300 years ago. But it's an accurate description of the social media – sometimes known in my language as the social mental media – long before it came into existence.

> '有不虞之誉, 有求全之毁': There are unexpected praises as there are scathing criticisms.

All I have to do to make it relevant today is to add a few more words to the whole sentence:

> There are unexpected praises as there are scathing criticisms, in the form of silence or indifference.

Whatever you post in there, there will always be total silence and indifference. But praises will come from the most unexpected people, from time to time.

Right now, I have received seven 'Likes' from someone I don't know on Instagram.

Reading Eastern Slope Su when '乱山'[36] appeared, for the first time, translatable. And I wrote down my instant translation in the margins: 'A mess of mountains'.

'A mess of hills', an afterthought, though not as good as the 'mm'.

♪♩♪

'the assault of memory', 'being chosen and criminal', 'the captives of daytime logic', 'flourishes and chaff', 'contemporary with the whole future', 'to love bores', 'a grotesque volcano', 'one of those flesh-and-blood ghosts', 'hateful in my own eyes'[37] – this is my way of quoting without quoting, fragmentary preferred over wholesale.

♪♩♪

And another poetic felicity that goes, '一溪风月', 'a creek of wind and moon', in my instant translation.[38]

And I forgot to say that the poem containing these words Eastern Slope Su wrote on a pillar of the bridge in an early morning after he woke up from a drunken sleep by the creek, as he reveals in a pre-poem note.

♪♩♪

It's best to remain unread than read with incomprehension or dismissal. And from here onwards, I do not put down the date and time when I write something. To date is to be dated.

♪♩♪

Recently, a harrowing voice that keeps accusing me, 'You have not taken any active part in any political protests against all the wrongs of the world. You have not openly supported all those who need support. You have not expressed any opinions of yours on any of the prominent social media outlets, such as FB, Twitter, Instagram, WeChat et cetera. You are so selfish! You don't have a public purpose in life.'

Then this:

> To shake people up, to wake them from their sleep, while knowing you are committing a crime and that it would be a thousand times better to leave them alone, since when they wake, too, you have nothing to offer them…[39]

'Yes, I am selfish,' I said to the voice. 'But that is fine.'

A thought: perhaps I should include some of the cuts from my latest novel as part of the self-censorship even though no one has accepted it because it has not even been submitted?

Oh, yes, I remember what it was that I was going to do but forgot to do along the way. It was a poem I spoke into my phone that got turned into characters while I was taking an early morning walk alone outside, as follows:

已经很久很久了，我只想离去。不知有什么办法能使人，从 120 斤变成，一粒灰尘。 不知有什么办法能使人，在一次做梦中彻底消失。每天每天每天都这样活着，实在没有没有没有意思。我只想把东西越快清除越好，不想留下任何痕迹。从这儿划一 道线，认定我不过只是一句行诗走鯀而已。

If you say you don't understand, I'm afraid I can't help you. Let's leave it there until you understand.

An editor in China wrote in reply today to my query about the possible publication of a book I wrote, as follows:

这几年我们有很多党建方面的出版任务，其他方面的书不怎么出了，请见谅。而且受经济大环境影响，现在图书市场不太好，目前大都是自费出书

You are lucky because right now I am in a good mood, conducive to translating this for your sake that goes,

I'm sorry but over the next few years, we focus on publishing books on Party construction and won't publish a lot of other books. And as a result of the Big Environment, the book market right now is not in a good way. At the moment, it's all self-published books.

The Big Environment (大环境) is normally rendered as 'the social, political and economic environment'.

Hopeless. But.

My posting of a photograph on Instagram showing white fallen flowers strewing the ground next to a short walk out on a footpath drew an immediate response from an admirer who clicked 'Like' with a comment, in Chinese: 花落不知多销.

I responded to that with this that goes, 'Hahaha n that translates into not knowing how many fallen flowers can be for sale.'

Without trying to explain it more than necessary, it suffices to say that this is a well-quoted line from an ancient Chinese poem to the effect that one does not know how many flowers have fallen during the rainy night. But the Instagram commentator quoted it wrongly, turning '花落知多少' into '花落不知多销'。

Still, it makes interesting wrong sense.

Before I go to sleep, I usually read five to six books, including my favourite Su Shi, in bed. If anyone gets read in bed, that's my best respect paid.

Then I saw this, once again, where the line goes, '家童鼻息已雷鸣。' Oh, how I love it! I can almost hear the boy snoring in a thunder-like noise inside a locked house. I found my translation of the poem, published years ago in a collection of ancient Chinese poems. It's here:

Listening to the river

> Written in Chinese by Su Shi (1037–1101)
> Translated into English by Ouyang Yu (1955–)

i wake up and get drunk again, drinking at eastern slope it's near midnight on my return home
my houseboy is snoring like thunder
unresponsive to my knocks on the door
leaning on my stick, i listen to the river

for long i resent the fact that i'm not master of my fate
why can't i just forget about it all?
on this quiet night with no wind, all ripples erased from the river
i wish i could disappear in my tiny little boat
and spend the rest of my life with rivers and seas

I'm beginning to like this guy if only for what he said here and I quote,

> They all write as though they wanted their personal monument. And I'm not just talking about their relation to the patrie, but to humanity, to society, to every manifestation of life. These writers are all so appallingly affirmative. They reinforce their readers in their bourgeois – i.e., antiquated – attitudes, instead of destroying as many of them as possible.[40]

I think I understand where he's coming from, although I don't like the way some writers in this country attack the PM as freely as they like on social media. After all, the PM is an ordinary bloke like every one of us. If you get rid of him, you'll have another PM. Constantly attacking and disliking every new PM doesn't render you more heroic and likeable. Rather, it makes you silly and pathetic.

In that well-known spat with the Americans, led by Antony Blinken, a few days ago, Yang Jiechi said something so unforgettable that days after I can still remember it word for Chinese word: *Women ba nimen xiang de tai hao le* (我们把你们想得太好了).

I remember it for two things, one that the official translation is not quite right that goes, 'We thought too well of the United States.'

If translated word for word, with the undertone, that would be something like this: 'We have been thinking too well of you.' Or 'We've had too high an opinion of you.' Or even 'We should never have held you in such high esteem.'

And the other reason I keep it so fast in my memory is the sadness of the remark, as it can only come from someone who wishes to be well treated and reciprocated in according the highest respect to the other party. And it, by accident, conveys something that I, as a migrant to Australia, have also been often thinking of: we have thought too highly of Australia to the degree that, in retrospect, it's not worth our efforts to even migrate to it in the first place and stay on.

What is unsaid in that remark is just that: you (the USA) are not really worth us thinking that highly of you.

A couple of days ago, I received comments back from S on my latest novel, previously known as AS. Among other things, she pointed out that it's 'Ouyang speaking', not the character. I responded by saying it's pointless to completely conceal yourself because, after all, it was all me, the characters of mine all having my blood running through their veins. No point pretending otherwise.

Then, at night and in bed, I read something by Samuel that echoes mine except that he did that more than a hundred years ago. He says,

> Every man's work, whether it be literature or music or pictures or architecture or anything else, is always a portrait of himself, and the more he tries to conceal himself the more clearly will his character appear in spite of him.[41]

That's it, hey. I love it.

Coincidences abound. During the day, I read 'Foure thousand winter thought he not too long', in one of the 'Anonymous Lyrics of the Fifteenth Century' by Adam Lay I-bounden.[42]

And at night I read Su Shi, with his line that goes, '百年里，浑教是醉，三万六千场。'[43] Meaning? If you get drunk 360 times a year, you'd end up getting drunk 36,000 times in a century.

I have never thought that China had helped Australia during the Second World War until I saw this that, just as the Japanese were on the point of invading Australia, 'the stout fighting of the Chinese…effectively prevented a Japanese invasion of white Australia in the Second World War'.⁴⁴

Shouldn't Australia have felt thankful to China for that?

The more I read Mencius, the less I like the rules he set for the common humanity because they sound too good to be true and too impracticable to work. It prompted me to write in the margins of the book featuring his quotes in Chinese, 'No rules hold long however good they are,' as Z, a priest friend of mine told me over yum cha a few days ago how Catholic rules were so good at the start for the priests to stay celibate, keeping them closer to God and having no fears of personal property through marriage, only to lead to all sorts of crime, including those against young boys.

I wonder, too, if there is something that deliberately balances things up, good against the bad, et cetera, so if you have very good intentions, they may lead to disasters.

Fifteen days ago, I wrote about 'being' as one of the most ridiculous concepts in Chinese and this view had been confirmed years ago by a Romanian-French friend – I call anyone a friend I can closely identify with spiritually, philosophically, linguistically, literarily and poetically,

> Whether it is spoken by a grocer or a philosopher, the word 'being', apparently so rich, so tempting, so charged with significance, in fact means nothing at all; incredible that a man in his right mind can use it on any occasion whatever.⁴⁵

Heidegger dismissed, although I think I'll persist a bit longer with his *Being and Time*, or 《病 and Time》 .

I like Pinter. That's more than enough said. Before I say more, I'll include a poem I just found, as follows:

Dance or how won

An old friend, a bum or
if you prefer, an itinerant musician
having returned to spend some time with his parents

in the Ardennes, was provoked
by some trifle to quarrel with his mother, a retired schoolteacher
just as she was getting ready to go to Mass

Beside herself, mute and pale, she flung
down her hat, her coat, then her blouse, her skirt
her underwear and stockings, and stark naked

performed a lascivious dance
before her horrified husband
and son pressed against the wall, incapable of stopping her with a
    gesture, a word

The performance over
she collapsed into a chair
and burst into sobs.

(Note: this is a found poem from E.M. Cioran's *Drawn and Quartered*. New York: Arcade Publishing, 2012 [1971], p. 69)

With Pinter, it's what he said about poets that caught my attention while pissing into the toilet. He says, or one of his characters says,

> The same thing applied to the poets. They were guilty of a criminal defection. He must impress upon her that the act of writing was the act of committing yourself to yourself. Consequently it was a moral question. The poets about them were signing their own death warrant each time they signed their name. Their work was not selfexpression so much as self-creation. And all that issued forth was a lie. Each poem they wrote was nothing more than a posthumous fart. The labour of dead men, who could only give birth to a corpse, in their own image. It was a debasement and sellout of

the purpose of writing, active only in that it delighted in its own smell.⁴⁶

How farting true!

They say this separator is a sign of music. To me, it looks like three high-heeled shoes put together, in a musical way.

And the poem I got smashed in 'Otherland 原乡砸诗群' is this:

《忠言》

如果你什么都做不了
也什么都做不好

那就做诗人吧

A self-translation by me goes,

Advice

If you are not good at doing anything
Or can do nothing well if you do do anything

Then become a poet.

Among others, an artist group member by the name of Chaos comments, saying,

诗人，在我的字典里是：研究自己溃败的人

And my translation of that is,

Poets, in my dictionary, are researchers of their own failures.

'Brilliant,' I commented back. I'll talk about poetry smashing when I have time.

♪♪

I thought of China's series of actions against the West. It can all be summariszed in two Chinese words: 学坏 and 还嘴。

学坏 (xue huai) literally means to learn bad. In the past, it's always the West that attacked China from its moral high ground, picking on her for all sorts of things, from human rights to political corruption. China listened and offered to improve its situation.

Not any more. They have learnt bad, to be bad, to do it the bad way, attacking back by picking on the West for its human rights record, Australia with its atrocities committed against the Aboriginals, and all the rest of them for their dirty bums that remain uncleaned.

The way to do this is to 还嘴 (huan zui), answering back, talking back or retorting, not what China used to be doing but more and more its new ways, all because it has learnt bad, to be bad, to be as bad as the West, picking on the rest of the world while ignoring one's own problems at home.

Then, when I went to the loo and opened this book, something came into view,

…the fact that we're about to have World War Three…[47]

That seems exactly what has been occupying my mind over the last few days.

♪♪

In all seriousness he says,

Being lies in the fact that something is, and in its Being as it is; in Reality; in presence-at- hand; in subsistence; in validity; in Dasein; in the 'there is'.[48]

I laughed and paused on the first two words, 'Being lies', then the rest of it.

I couldn't help blurting out with this admiration that goes, 个狗日的，太厉害了! when I read what he said below:

I have followed only one idea all the way – the idea that everything man achieves necessarily turns against him.⁴⁹

I don't want to cite examples to prove his point. I know. My question is, how did he know?

Then he says,

One does not write because one has something to say but because one wants to say something.⁵⁰

And my immediate response is,

写作的目的，不是为了被读，而是为了被写、为了写出来。

My self-translation:

One writes not for the purpose of being read but for the purpose of being written, of writing out.

Finished reading *The Virtue of Yin: Studies on Chinese Women*, by Lily Xiao Hong Lee, yesterday. Most impressed with the first part of the article on Helen Quach the conductor. But wondered why she didn't make it big in the Western part of the world, including Australia. Was that because she was Asian?

Checked into Wikipedia just now. Found two things she said that interested me, one about herself:²⁷

I have a choleric temperament, kept well under control – forceful when I conduct, but very quiet and ready to listen when away from my baton. I am a woman. I like a lot of personal attention…

And the other about her not getting married:

I just never met anyone that I wanted to share my life permanently with…⁵¹

I think of my aunt in a novel I have not written.

40

Asians and Caucasians, or more relevantly, Cauc/asians, are at the two extremes from one another. When Samuel writes in his novel that people in that place were 'tolerators, if not lovers, of all that was familiar, haters of all that was unfamiliar',[52] I wished I had been like that thirty years ago. I, along with my friends and people I knew, in my former country, were haters of all that was familiar and lovers of all that was unfamiliar, which is exactly why we ended up overseas, permanently caught in the unfamiliar that is familiar that will remain forever unfamiliar.

When I saw the nickname, 'Dollar a Word',[53] the first Chinese equivalent that came to me is 金口难开 (*jin kou nan kai*), a gold mouth hard to open.

As someone originally born and bred in China, I have always been under the impression that Chinese people are worse in everything than their white counterparts if not as bad as them.

Henry Handel Richardson's *The Getting of Wisdom*, in its portrait of the girl Laura Rambotham as 'a footlicker' (p. 182), and 'a very double-faced child' (p. 184), who 'learnt to weigh her words before uttering them, instead of blurting out her thoughts in the childish fashion that had exposed her to ridicule;…to keep her real opinions to herself, and to make those she expressed tally with her hearers',[54] helps me see that human beings are essentially the same regardless of their cultural, religious, ethnic and racial, even gender backgrounds.

In fact, I don't need that to see that because I have seen enough to prove the point. Still, it's good to see Australians getting so complicated in a novel, written by a woman using a male name.

Zhang Huaimin, Su Shi's contemporary, was an official in the Northern Song dynasty and was demoted and sent into exile in Huangzhou, my hometown. They became close friends there. Su wrote a prose piece in memory of a night they spent together and here I'll provide a translation of it:

On a Night Visit to Chengtian Temple

On the night of October 12th, in the sixth year of Yuanfeng, I shed my clothes and was about to turn in when the moonlight shone through the door. I rose and took a delightful walk. Thinking there was no one to enjoy the night together, I went to visit Zhang Huaimin at Chengtian Temple. He hadn't turned in, either. We walked side by side in the courtyard. The ground of the courtyard was as bright and hollow as a pool of water, with interweaving water plants and floating hearts, actually shadows of the bamboos and cypresses. What night doesn't have the moon? Where doesn't one find bamboos and cypresses? But nowhere can one find such a leisurely two as you and I.

I must say I love this, not the least because I had many similar experiences in China when young; also because the country I'm currently living in now is never the one for that. Never.

To re-experience it, I have to go back to the town of exiles again, my Huangzhou.

♪♪

I want to write something that is uncategorisable. Call this fiction. Call this ficnonfiction. Call it transfiction. Call it transpoeticnonfiction. Call it anything but.

♪♪

先河: first river。

In the process of learning from the West, including learning how to behave badly, and as badly, China initiated its own retaliatory sanctions on the USA, Canada and the UK, something that seemed the US's privileges and sole right to impose on the rest of the world in the past without any country daring to hit back.

In this, China has 开了先河, opened the first river. Dig that, a Chinese expression.

Allow me not to make any explanations. If you understand, you do. If you don't, you don't.

♪♪

On the scrap paper that I wrote down the idea for the above, I noticed a short poem I wrote sometime ago:

In Australia, democracy is a poorly managed
Self-deception

And I also wrote a Chinese couplet underneath the couplet above,

爬倒后
你就别想再跌起来了

Dates and time recorded in handwriting but not included here.

♪♪

He says,

If we did not bear the stigmata of life, how easy it would be to steal away, and how well everything would go by itself!⁵⁵

In my reading, the word 'stigmata' became 'age spots' as I thought, I've written a poem about that. Let me go and find it. Right, here it goes:

《黑斑》

人们说
这是老人斑

我在五十岁的时候
看见它出来

就再也不走了
我怀疑

它跟道德有关
但我找不到证据

我用手在镜子上抹了一把
擦掉了黑斑

但我无论走到哪里
都能在人们眼中看到

曾经作恶的
痕迹

(2007年9月7号夜晚10点18分写于Canberra Florey的床上)

My self-translation, without bothering explaining how I came to write it and all that sort of shit:

Dark Spots

They say
These are old people's spots

I saw them out
And refuse to go

When I reached 50
And I wondered

If they have anything to do with morality
But I can't find any evidence

I wiped the mirror with my hand
And removed the dark spots

But wherever I go
I can see the traces

Of having committed the evil
In the eyes of the people

(translated 12.04 p.m., Sunday 28 March 2021, at home in K)

I wrote two poems just now. One is 'Just now'.

《Just now》

我会长时间地看着天空
看那些云
那些一动也不动
映着余晖的云
它们的大面积堆叠
它们的木然、漠然和云然
我转身回屋、关门
意识到，我所说的"长时间"
连一分钟都不到

(7.15 p.m., Sunday 28/3/2021, at home in K)

And the other is as follows:

7.16 p.m.

Whatever they say about you and how hard they are running you down
This is something I must say before I die:

You twice gave me a professorship
While australia didn't even give me a job

In the 30 years I have lived in it
What a country is *that*

Compared with you
China?

(7.20 p.m., Sunday 28/3/2021, at home in K)

♪♪

This is what I'm going to say in an email to be sent to a writer friend:

> Hi, Bla-bla-bla-bla, I'm writing something I have never done before, a something that I mean to write before I die. I don't write it to appeal to anyone. I don't even write it for publication. I certainly don't write it to a country that only likes praises. I'll speak my mind as honestly as I can and die.

As soon as the idea came across my mind, I gave it up.

♪♪

In *The Way of All Flesh*, I caught a plagiariser red-handed, who

> cuts little bits out of the Bible and gums them with exquisite neatness by the side of other little bits; this he calls making a Harmony of the Old and New Testaments. Alongside the extracts he copies in the very perfection of hand-writing extracts from Mede... Patrick, and other old divines. (p. 67)

His name is Theobald. In today's terms, he's only doing 'Copy/ Paste'.

♪♪

I chuckled to myself when I read,

> We were young. We accepted that sometime in the course of our lives we would probably get married, but we felt similarly about the arterial sclerosis that would probably befall us in twenty or thirty years as well. (*The Emperor's Tomb*, p. 17)

I thought back, not of marriage as something I had looked forward to in my twenties, but the future down the years, twenty or thirty years down the track, something so horrible because there was no new prospect as if you could see it through right to the boring end.

For that simple reason, I gave up my good job as a translator and interpreter to pursue MA studies in Shanghai, then PhD studies in Australia, an absolute strategic error, I dare say. But who can predict the future?

♪♪

In *A New History of the Irish in Australia*, which I bought in March 2019 in Dublin, what I remember most clearly is this advertisement that says, 'No Irish Need to Apply', along with other anti-Irish attitudes that reminded of the ones against the Chinese.

It is for this reason that I took note when I came across this description of a character, Mr C., in *Don't Talk To Me About Love* by Craig McGregor that goes,

> His face, beneath the grey, short-napped hair, was an Irish-Catholic exercise in asymmetry, a nose stuck on here, an ear there, one side noticeably more lined than the other. (Penguin Books, 1972, p. 60)

I, though, have a lot of good things to say about the Irish people, mostly good.

♪♪

When I heard Cioran say that 'the dead speak the same language as the living, except that for them words have a meaning contrary to the one they had' (*The Trouble with Being Born*, p. 210), I was on the point of citing a number of examples to show that the 'complete reversal of language' actually exists between the Chinese language and the English when I read something in *Claiming a Continent* that indicates that even between the Great Britain and Australia, such reversals exist. See this here:

> While the defeats in Greece, Crete and Singapore caused British political and military leaders to question the bravery of Australian soldiers, these same defeats were held up for Australians as further examples of Anzac courage. (David Day, p. 294)

I heard my own voice coming from years ago on ABC in answer to a question about my novel *Billy Sing* (2017):

> What they celebrated year in and year out is a total failure. And that's what the book is about, too.

The rest of it is forgotten.

🎵🎵

As soon as I saw 'delusions of persecution' in Freud's *Totem and Taboo* (p. 50), I recalled how those refugees I helped interpret for at such organisations as RRT (Refugee Review Tribunal) years ago were trying to create all sorts of stories of persecution meted out to them in China and some could even get Chinese police stations to produce certificates in support of their claims.

This is 'delusions of persecution' for a purpose.

🎵🎵

Not long after I talked about Theobald's plagiarism in *The Way of All Flesh*, I bumped into this: 'Existing is plagiarism' (*Drawn and Quartered*, p. 74); and immediately followed it with a two-word comment: 好玩! (good fun).

🎵🎵

Cioran says,

> No one more useless, and more unusable, than I: a datum I must quite simply accept, without taking any pride in the fact whatever.' (*The Trouble with Being Born*, pp. 210–1)

I commented,

他所有哲学的出发点。我们相同：我有用却不被用。像父亲。

You, my reader, are lucky because I am not yet dead and can provide a self-translation when I am in the mood. It goes,

(That's) the departing point of all his philosophy. We are alike: I am useful but not used. Like (my) father.

When Father was alive, he compared himself to a chamber pot, picked up when needed and put aside when not, a typical attitude of the Party and the government towards useful people from the old days.

🎵🎵

'Might as well,' I heard myself say. I was telling myself to record the poems I wrote in the margins of *The Trouble with Being Born* whenever poetry struck in the middle of reading it. I normally record it or them elsewhere. But I put them here today, Chinese or English, regardless.

越是都多的时候
越要学会少

(2021.2.18 上午拉尿时写)

跟你说，等你的书成了世界名著
你早就不在世上了

(2021.3.13 床上 9.34pm)

鲁迅是一种黑暗的力量
一种发光的黑暗力量

Cioran 更是，他的悲观使人更有力量
悲观而不悲观

(2021.3.19 夜洗脚时)

did we award them for virginity? what is quality?
does it equate with money?
the better the more sales?
y do we go for youth?
does youth mean money?
does youth equate with quality? does it equate with success?
r we ashamed of ourselves
for being aged?

(2.53 p.m., 8/1/2021, on tram bk home)

🎵🎵

Just wrote an email to E, a curator, as follows:

Hi E-,
    I was having a chat with a friend just now when I said something that my writer friend said I could put down as an explanation

of my single-copy concept, so I wrote it down and thought it might help you, too, in understanding where I came from.

> I don't want to give birth to a million copies. All I ever want is one single copy published to mark your rejection. If you don't want to publish it for others to read it, I'll make it available for time to read it for time alone has time.

> Not exactly my words, but something like that, from my memory.
> Best,
> Ouyang
> https://youyang2.blogspot.com

If there is a smell of 'Man' as Cioran puts it here that goes, 'Man gives off a special odor: of all the animals, he alone smells of the corpse' (*The Trouble with Being Born*, p. 208), there must be a smell generated of countries, too, PC of Australia and PIC of China.

If you want to censor the past, you probably have to censor this old English poem. Titled 'I Have a Gentle Cock', the poem ends with the line that goes, 'And every night he percheth him / In my lady's chamber.'[56]

I recalled a friend's poem in which a woman asks her man to come home inside her. It can't be published. But it can be written, if only for himself. Or for me.

Some of the things said can be turned into instant poetry, such as this:

> Can I go to some third country – Albania, maybe – and write another book?[57]

A found poem, now:

> Can I go
> to some third
> country – Albania

maybe – and
write
another book?

Thank you, my thought, that came to me early this morning and suggested a title for a new piece that I am going to write:

'An Angry China that Answers Back'

As to who I should write it for, I am not sure. But I *am* sure about a poem I learnt decades ago as part of military tactics, known as a sixteen-character rhyming formula for guerrilla warfare,

敌进我退，敌驻我扰，敌疲我打，敌退我追

And Mao's slogan, which is actually a more fitting one,

人不犯我，我不犯人；人若犯我，我必犯人

My translation below, only of Mao's slogan, also sixteen characters:

We won't attack unless attacked. We will attack if attacked.

This morning's news about the sacking of Jeremy Cordeaux, who said a 'silly girl who got drunk' (see here: https://www.news.com.au/entertainment/tv/radio/veteran-adelaide-radio-host-jeremy-cordeaux-sacked-over-brittany-higgins-tirade/news-story/e4a351373860af6e3cee6b2cfec bb74a) elicited an immediate response from me as I recalled the saying by Mencius: 洁身自好, literally, keeping the body clean and keeping to oneself.

One online source puts it thus, slightly altered by me:

Lead an honest and clean life while refusing to be contaminated by evil influences.[58]

All I may add to that is, if you don't, you might.

♪𝄐♪

Three days ago, I received a rejection of a fairly big novel manuscript of mine and I emailed my reply with a 'Please remove my ms from your file. Thank you.'

    The publisher has so far not bothered replying.

♪𝄐♪

I won't show the whole passage again when I 'found' another poem, such as this one, from Patrick White's *The Living and the Dead*, an almost inexhaustible source of poetry or found poetry, such an impossible fiction:

> **'You**
>
> went down out
> of the street
> through a glass
> tunnel
>
> Your head, your body
> so many identical
> heads
> on so many identical
>
> bodies blossomed
> in recurrent bouquets
> around
> above'[59]

(10.53 a.m., Tuesday 30/3/2021, at home in K)

♪𝄐♪

If you think I'm boastful, that's your problem, not mine. I'll keep going.

    Something from a book I'm reading, along with dozens of other ones:

> Mental telepathy – it is the way humans were designed to communicate. Different languages and various written alphabets are eliminated as obstacles when people use head-to-head talk.

But it would never work in my world, I reasoned, where people steal from the company, cheat on taxes, have affairs. My people would never stand for being literally 'open-minded.' There is too much deception, too much hurt, too much bitterness to hide.

...

The Real People don't think the voice was designed for talking...[60]

Something emerged from the depths of my memory from seventeen years ago, on 19 August. After remaining restless and worried for days about my younger brother in prison for Falun Gong-related crimes, I decided to ring his father-in-law, whom I had not spoken to for years. As soon as he picked up the phone, the first thing he said was, 'We are waiting for you!'

What happened was Ming, my brother, had been released from jail the day before. But he had disappeared, probably gone to live with a Falun Gong practitioner friend and nowhere to be found. Both of us hoped that things might get better and we'd see him pretty soon.

The next day, a call came from Father-in-law: Ming is dead, at the age of forty-one, as a result of the persecution of Falun Gong practitioners by the government.

I had never believed in telepathy. But I have since.

Someone approached me and made an offer. He wanted to interview me for a major national radio station. I preferred an email interview. He wanted a phone interview because radio. I got him to call me and fill me in with more details. When he called, I was driving. We talked. The more we talked, the less I liked it. There was no payment. I had to spend at least thirty minutes doing work for him. There was no prospect of selling a single book of mine. And I would be in a podcast for free access by all and sundry. The point? Conclusion: I have to be selfish. I have learnt to be selfish from this country, learning bad, remember?

Back at home, I wrote a poem for myself,

4.27 p.m.

There isn't much to be proud of isn't there
30 years after one's first arrival in this country
when they still refer to you as a 'migrant'
and hope to give you an interview
about your 'migrant' experience
why not simply replace the word with something like
'prisoner', a prisoner of time
of a country that has made sure that one will never be
a newspaper or magazine editor
a company manager, a university
professor, not even a lecturer, not even a seasonal, casual instructor
is it their intention to get you to work for them for free
by providing information they need of you –
what's the point of wasting your breaths in speaking your mind
to a total stranger
all he ever wants is to imprison you
in his nice radio work
for him to get paid
while you are accessible
in an eternal podcast –
no, I'm going to say no
wait till tomorrow

(done at 4.37 p.m., Tuesday 30/3/2021, at home in K)

Interim report: I have just unfollowed three people on Instagram.

'I wonder why you keep referring to me as "migrant". We have been in this country for thirty years now and have been this country's citizens since 1998. If we are migrants, who are not migrants? To keep doing that is to keep putting us down.' I recalled saying this to the radio guy over the phone while driving and then saying to my wife at home, who didn't like the idea of the interview, either, 'The more you speak your mind, the more they like it because that's exactly what they want from you and for nothing. I'm not going to do that. If they ask for a donation, I might donate a few dollars. But I'm not donating my feelings and thoughts to an institution bent on digging the goldmine of your mind for free. Plus I don't feel comfortable speaking to total strangers about how I truly feel and think. I've already told him that and that I won't be agreeing with the mainstream things.'

♪♪

Came across the word 'nothing' when I thought, that's a present progressive tense: 'noth' and 'ing'.

I met the word in Pinter's *Dwarfs*, p. 62.

♪♪

'Encyclopedia' is a nickname that refers to one who 'has all the answers'.[61]

Mom came back in that instant, saying as she did before on many occasions when I was a teenager, 'Your dad is a genius in mathematics. His classmates called him "几何学词典", a dictionary of geometry, and would consult him whenever they had difficulties solving problems.'

♪♪

Saw something I liked and keep it here:

Aesthetics of Obituary[62]

To avoid the clichés
Of the obituary writers,
Die in obscurity.
A fine bed in a light-filled room
Someone who adores you is at your side
And vowed to silence.

And, we happened to discuss where and how to get ourselves buried afterwards with a friend who visited me late in the morning in my home to get a copy of my novel translated and published in Catalan.

♪♪

Saw this by Mencius:

养生者，不足以当大事，惟送死可以当大事。

And my quick rendering,

Keeping one's parents alive is not as big a thing as seeing them off at death.

♪♪

Reading 《西游记》 (*Journey to the West*, a sixteenth-century Chinese novel) late in my life, having read it as a teenager, I saw the expression '自由自在' again and once again realised my dissatisfaction with its equivalent to the English 'freedom'.

To be 自由, literally, is to let self, translated in a reversal of the language. And to be 自在 is to be at self, which is why I once rendered the expression as 'let self at self'.

The essence of a foreigner's unhappiness in a foreign country is not that he is not free; he could be free at the cost of being a freak, or freek, but that he can't let his self at self.

How can you let a divided self at self or let a self at a divided self?

♪♪

无聊, or boredom, is one theme that constantly resurfaces in my poetry, written either in Chinese or in English, right from the 1980s.

I like it even more because I now have Cioran's support as he said,

To that friend who tells me he is bored because he cannot work, I answer that boredom is a higher state, and that we debase it by relating it to the notion of work. (*Drawn and Quartered*, p. 78)

A higher state, indeed!

♪♪

'Waiting for the offer,' I finished the conversation between A and me, with a flash of my hand, invisible to him about 140 kilometres away.

'That's a good title,' he said.

Days after, when the fragment of that conversation came back, I thought, why not change the title of this book in progress from *Book of Connections* or *It Could Also Be Called 'Bits and Pieces'* into *Book of Connections* or *Waiting for the Offer*?

Done.

In 《临皋闲题》 ('An idler's title for Lingao'), Su Shi writes,

> A dozen steps down Lingao Pagoda is the Big River. Half of it contains the snow water from Mount Emei. I eat and drink from it. I use it for taking a bath. What need do I have for returning home? If there never is an owner of the rivers, mountains and the moon, the idler is then the owner.[63]

I love this and I translated it; it used to be *my* river and *my* hometown.

Life is a series of balances. You win, you lose. You die, you gain a new birth. You have too much money, your problems pile up.

Straight into a mini-tale. In Wenling, Zhejiang, China, a few years ago, we went boating and fishing, us a group of poets, with another group of common tourists. They had the first net drawn, a full net of fish. That took us until eight p.m. when our net, the second one, was drawn. The net was broken, not a single fish caught.

Is this God's will? Or is that heaven's punishment meted out towards the poets? No. It's neither planned nor intended. It's just a balance. They had a full net. We had an empty net. That's all there is to it.

That's what I recalled when I read this, by Freud:

> …the ceremonial taboo of kings is ostensibly the highest honour and protection for them, which actually is a punishment for their exaltation, a revenge taken on them by their subjects. (*Totem and Taboo*, p. 51)

Unlike my tale, this is the balance of the bad and the good in one, relentlessly.

♪♪

Just finished reading *Idlers in the Land*, by Keith Thomas, without much impression except its not-impressive portrait of the Aborigines. No more comments.

At the same time, I like what an Aboriginal leader says in *Mutant Message Down Under*:

> Humans cannot exist if everything that is unpleasant is eliminated instead of understood. (Marlo Morgan, p. 69)

Mosquitoes, I remember, used to be a source of nuisance, and poetry, to me when I lived in China. Now, long time no see.

♪♪

Months ago, at the height of the pandemic, a friend rang and checked on me. 'Are you safe?'

I said, ' I'm having a walk outside. It's been quite okay. But I turn my head back from time to time, just in case, you know. But nothing has happened so far.'

It's not till today that I realisd something essential that I have failed to notice. And I wrote a poem about it.

No one bashed me outside in the open

Nor pushed me onto the ground from behind
Nor spat me in the face
Nor gave me Chinese burns
Nor twisted my arms behind me
Nor stared hard at me
Nor spoke to me
Nor made death threats over the phone
Nor made such threats over the email
Nor chucked stones in my direction when I walked in the park
Nor pointed at me
Nor sicced a dog on me

Nor pulled my non-existent pigtails
Nor pulled back their eyes at me
Nor abused me in yet another fuck word

Nothing ever happened except few clicked 'Like' again after Covid-19

(7.46 p.m., Wed, 31/3/2021)

♪♪

I just found this. Don't ask me how. It goes,

妻不如妾，妾不如婢，婢不如妓，妓不如偷，偷得着不如偷不着。

And my translation:

Wives are not as good as concubines; concubines are not as good as maids; maids are not as good as whores; whores are not as good as stolen goods (the ones to have by stealth) and stolen goods are not as good as goods impossible to steal (the ones hard to come by).

It's from a Ming novel: 《雪涛小说》.

♪♪

'If no one interviews me, I shall interview myself.' This is the thought that went across my mind just now.

I have done a number of self-interviews already, since the early 1980s. But I'm not inclined to show them here. Why would I?

♪♪

If a writer's words are any guide, short fiction as a genre has reached the point of extinction. One has little time for it. An A4 page of poetry takes much less time than a short story, plus the fact that one doesn't have to worry about the intricate human relationship involved in the story. I like Raymond Carver because of the brevity and poetry of his prose. Too many others are like muddied waters that can be dispensed with in one go.

♪♪

Poetry is at its most inhumane when it turns deliberately obscure and murky, often designed to win favours of the judging panels for literary awards.

♪♪

Two things Kenneth Koch wrote I like and dislike.[64] The one I like is,

Aesthetics of Poetry and Prose

Chekhov told Bunin
Not to begin writing
Until he felt as cold as ice.
Keats wrote to Shelley
'I am a fever of myself!'

And the one I don't like is,

Aesthetics of Fiction

Don't write stories
That have no plot
And have no characters
And have no style.

And shortly after I read these two, I saw my own poem, written on 19/6/2004, in a book I'm editing of my Chinese poems written between 2000 and 2009. It goes,

由于不会
他把小说写成了诗
把诗写成了半小说

Interested readers are encouraged to use Google Translate.

♪♪

Writing has been made so reader-friendly that it's like the best laxative or semen-inducing porn.

🎵

Editing of my book, continuously, with a title that defies translation: 《更的的》.

Just found a poem I wrote,

艺术

所有最好的作品
皆于失败时写成

(2003 年 12 月 18 日星期四)

You are lucky because I'm in the mood. Hence my self-translation:

Art

All the best works
Are written when one is a failure

🎵

There is nothing wrong to speak one's mind. The only thing wrong is to quote it exponentially for an ulterior motive.

🎵

Once a Chinese, always half a Chinese.

🎵

I saw another version of the early sixteenth-century English song of 'Western Wind', as follows:

Westron wynde, when wilt thou blow,
The small raine down can raine.
Cryst, if my love were in my armes
And I in my bedde again!

And all I can think of in tandem to that is 'Big Wind Song', composed by Liu Bang, the first emperor of the Han Dynasty, reigning in 202–195 BC, consisting of only three lines that Liu sang when drunk, hitting the Zhu, a percussion instrument as he sang,

大风起兮云飞扬
威加海内兮归故乡
安得猛士兮守四方

  Might I say that while 'Western wind' is pining for love, 'Big Wind Song' is the emperor wondering where he could secure brave soldiers to safeguard the borders, a private longing versus a national concern?

♪♪

I wrote, the other day, these words:

活着、活着
已经把自己活成了不可能

  And self-translated them:

Living till one turns
into an impossibility

♪♪

This morning, I heard the man say to his woman, 'Everyone is different in this world. Why do they expect others to be the same as them?'
  And the woman said, 'Right. Isn't freedom what you want? Why do you want to restrict others from freedom?'

♪♪

Yesterday morning, I was taking photographs of cockatoos on the lines when a man said, 'What are you doing?'
  I turned to see an old white man, standing in the footpath leading to his driveway, a roll of newspaper under his arm.
  'Oh, I'm taking a photo of them,' said I as I pointed upwards at the birds.
  'Are you from China?' the man asked.
  'Yes, but that's a long time ago, thirty years. I'm a citizen, like you.'
  'Sorry?'
  'I am an Australian citizen.'

'I see.' The man paused and said, 'Did you suffer any anti-Asian racism?'

'Not really, not personally. Why?'

'There are bad people everywhere.'

'I don't have a problem with Australians. They are friendly and they mind their own matters.'

'That's right.'

The conversation didn't end there as it wandered off to other subjects, such as reading and writing and the younger generation's addiction to their mobile phones.

It's not till I got home that I realised I ought to have said 'they mind their own business.'

A thought drifted into my mind: *Life's Little Ironies*. I checked Hardy and found the info. 'I'll buy a copy,' I said to myself even as my recent distaste for short fiction grew beyond my control.

And I remember what Cioran said about irony that I totally agree with:

> One struggles, one labors, one sacrifices, apparently for oneself, actually for anyone at all, for some future enemy, for an unknown enemy. And this is even truer of peoples than of individuals. Heraclitus was mistaken: it is not the lightning, but irony that rules the universe. It is irony that is the law of the world. (*Drawn and Quartered*, p. 80)

I hesitate to recommend anything I like in my readings. And I used to read nothing of the works in a list a friend strongly recommended to me.

I have an Italian friend F. In his world travels, including Europe, he always avoids the UK, never getting near its borders. His answer to my question is always a 'I don't like them.'

63

I have never understood why until recently when I came across something in David Day's book that says, 'Apart from [Second World] war refugees…an increasing proportion of European immigrants were unassisted immigrants from Italy, Greece and Yugoslavia, sources of immigration that Australia had largely distained in the past' and because of 'Italy's wartime alliance with Germany, Queensland had introduced a wartime ban on non-Britons buying land in that tropical state.' (*Claiming a Continent*, p. 304)

♪♪

I'll quote the following and translate it:

子曰：'予欲无言。' 子贡曰：'子如不言，则小子何述焉?' 子曰：'天何言哉？四时行焉，百物生焉，天何言哉？'

My translation below:

Confucius says, 'I don't want to speak any more.' Zi Gong says, 'If you don't speak any more, how can we learn?' Confucius says, 'Does the sky speak? Four seasons operate and things grow as usual. Does the sky speak?'

♪♪

If I am approached by someone in the future for a blurb about this book I'm writing, what would I say?

A rambler and idler's wildest dream come true.

Or perhaps, simply, 'I have no comments.' Put that as a blurb on the back cover please.

♪♪

Going through my poems written in the decade from 2000 to 2009, I met with one on the word 'being', a bilingual poem, which I wouldn't mind including here for my non-readers.

《谈 Being》

老百姓谈虎色变
一如中国学者谈 Being 变色
Being 是个什么东西?
它在英文中是人
如 human being

这是小菜一碟
哪有我的发明过硬、过瘾:
我说如今的人都是 human bin
不要把 being 和 bin 混为一谈
后者是垃圾桶
being 最简单,也最难译
颇像汉字的大饼
最常见、也最难译
可别译成 big cake
那是大蛋糕,要打屁股的
依我看,就译它成 big being
或者干脆译成: Da Being
管它是啥
只要能吃就行
回过头来再看 being
不就是一个 be, 再加上 ing
让"是"变成进行时
很有点儿像让汉语之口
一个劲儿说:是、是、是
进而言之
在当代汉语中
be 是一个下行的词
岂止如此, be 简直就是一个在下的词,而且很女
它从汉语之舌上滑下来时
就是一个简化的 b
管它大B还是小b
那是这个时代所有中国人休闲的去处
B 和 being
明白了吗?
也就是 B 加上 ing 的进行时

跟老子庄子墨子划子没关系
倒是 Da Being 或 Da Bing 更相宜

(2004年1月9日星期五)

Well, this one is easier, for those who want to research the origins of my bilingual or self-translated poetry:

日子过得很慢很慢
days drag slowly

欧阳昱

Ouyang Yu

日子过得很慢很慢。吃饭。圣诞。睡觉。抽烟。
Days drag slowly. Eating. Christmas. Sleeping. Smoking.
睡觉不是为了睡觉。睡觉为了做梦。早晨醒来不想起来。想再入梦境。
Sleeping not for sleeping. Sleeping for dreaming. Waking up in the morning, not wanting to get up. Wanting to get back into the dream.
吃饭。打呵欠。吐痰。抽烟。想让梦再来一遍。
Eating. Yawning. Spitting. Smoking. Wanting to have the dream again.
坐监。厕所瓷砖上照见一方被子和床铺。早上九点以后的阳光。羊年。
Sitting in prison. The toilet tile mirroring a corner of the quilt and the bed. Sunlight after 9 a.m. The year of goat. 很慢很慢。天就又要黑了。抬头窗的一角。那边。某人家的圣诞。光线。
Very very slowly. The day is getting dark. Raising my head to see a corner of the window. Yonder. Some family's Christmas. Light.
吃肉。吃鱼。吃烙饼。鸡蛋。圣诞。一夜一个电子邮件。慢慢的。
Eating meat. Eating fish. Eating fried cakes. Christmas. One email per night. Slowly.
一天三杯茶。四杯。或者五杯。看书。几本花着看。偶尔。青色网站。
Three cups of tea a day. Four cups. Or five cups. Reading books. Reading several mixedly. Occasionally. Green-coloured internet stations.

慢慢吃时间。时间无法拍电视。擤鼻涕。拉屎。吃。活得像个动物。

Slowly eating time. Time impossible to video. Blowing the nose. Shitting. Eating. Living like an animal.

是个动物。诗歌动物。栅栏那边。有一只榔头。在动。

Being an animal. Poetic animal. Beyond the fence. A hammer. Moving.

Duras 说。Literature is women。已经翻译了一遍。法译英。

Duras says. Literature is women. Already translated it once. French to English.

牛奶。Cereals。泡着六个"目"字。吃了三个下去。

Milk. Cereals. Soaking six characters of eyes. Eating three.

然后去拉。拿起一本书。周而复始。

Then going to shit. Picking up a book. Repeating the process.

(written in Chinese on 27/12/2002 and self-translated on 22/12/2003)

Facts that may not mean anything. But according to C, no girls from China that he dated and invited to dinner or coffee ever said 'thank you'.

Chinese Australian girls are different. They not only say 'thank you' but they rush ahead to pay.

裸葬。Luozang. Naked burial. Something I learnt of from a prose piece by Su Shi. A rich man by the name of Yang Wangsun, alive in the Western Han dynasty, advised his children to bury him naked so that his dead body was in physical contact with the earth.

Wonderful idea as I'm approaching that stage myself.

More info here: http://www.chinaknowledge.de/History/Han/personsyangwangsun.html

Du Fu says, 千秋万岁名, 寂寞身后事。

I translate: Fame of a thousand autumns but solitude post-life.

🎵

The episode of the bottle of water from Jordan broken in the cellar in *The Way of All Flesh* (p. 73) served to remind me of a story told by my dad years before his death that goes something like this.

A corrupt official has a party celebrating his birthday. He opens a bottle of Maotai, a precious gift from someone who bribed him in order to get a promotion. When the official opens the bottle and fills the cups for his friends with much pride, a pungent and putrid smell meets their noses. Soon enough, and to their horror, they find it not the real liquor but the yellowish piss.

The moral of the story? The man, having wasted much money and many efforts, had not got what he wanted, so he took it out on the official with the ingenious idea of the piss bottle.

An artist could do an artwork titled 'Piss Official' along the lines of 'Piss Christ'.

🎵

Fake news is another instance of bad learning. Whenever he didn't like anything he heard, Trump would say, 'Fake news!'

Now, that's exactly what China is doing whenever the West uploaded its attacks on its record. If you behave badly, people will learn to behave as badly as you.

🎵

Just wrote a poem, in the middle of having a shit:

《复活节》

云也放假了
走了、回家了、到别处云游去了

留下一个瓦蓝瓦蓝、湛蓝湛蓝
碧蓝碧蓝、blue、blue 的天空

和一个一大早就在天上
放哨的无花果状的月亮

(copied/revised at 9.24 a.m., Sunday 4/4/2021, at home in K, based on a handwritten draft done at third shit)

When I quoted Confucius as saying 'I don't want to speak any more', a song immediately started playing in my headtape, like it was a tape, the song titled, 'We don't talk any more.'

Then, Xun Yue's quoting the same Confucius remark as evidence how difficult it is to please a king, his twenty-four reasons including the obvious ones that if you criticise the king, you get punished; if you are too smart, the king hates you; if you speak in simple terms, the king looks down upon you; if you speak in highly technical and philosophical terms, the king gets offended because he doesn't understand, so on and so forth.

You think this only happened in Confucius's days? No. Nga, a writer friend, told me a similar story. On WeChat, he approaches an editor for the possibility of translating a book. In the meantime, he sees daily postings by the editor. He does not click likes. It's a difficult situation he finds himself in. If he clicks likes, the editor might think he's trying to please him because he wants to get the job. If he doesn't, he may think he doesn't like him. If he doesn't at first but changes his mind over time and does, the editor may think he is inconsistent.

In the end, the friend decides not to bother, awaiting in silence the impossibility of getting the book to translate.

More on Xun Yue: https://en.wikipedia.org/wiki/Xun_Yue

'Only stammerers are great poets in Germany.' (Joseph Roth, *A Life in Letters*, p. 62)

I thought of similar remarks made of poets or poetry in their respective countries. Lars in Denmark: 'Nothing much of Danish poetry is good.'

Nga in Australia: '99.99% of Chinese poetry is trash.'

♪♪

Goethe's poetry, translated into Chinese, is so dull that I began to pay particular attention to the footnotes about his relationships with various women and began to suspect that he must have had a lot of affairs that he wrote about in his poems in a very unopen way. But his poetry, not fantastic, not in the Chinese translation.

Now, I bumped into this about his *Faust*:

> ...a translation of Faust, which she read through, to the end of the First Part at least, with a kind of dreary wonder why such a dull thing should be called great. (*The Getting of Wisdom*, p. 190)

♪♪

I'm beginning to realise that I've run out of all my chances in Australia. To remain longer here, or there, is to remain more posthumous.

Then I saw this, a remark by Alan Moorhead:

> To stay at home [in Australia] was to condemn yourself to nonentity. (Quoted in *Claiming a Continent*, p. 322)

And I felt better. After all, I can't go anywhere else now. High time I awarded myself with the status of a nonentity.

♪♪

Did he talk about me when he said the following:

> Out of therapeutic concern, he had put into his books everything in himself that was impure, the residue of his thought, the dregs of his mind. (*Drawn and Quartered*, p. 85)

♪♪

Perhaps a local Aboriginal leader's words to a woman from New York might be a cooling agent for the hot heads of the Australian government in its policies towards China at the moment:

> We do not understand, agree, or accept your ways, but we do not

judge. We honour your position. You are where you are supposed to be, given your past choices and your current free will to make decisions. This place serves for us the same as other sacred sites. It is a time to pause, to reflect, to confirm our relationship to Divine Oneness and all life. There's nothing left here, you see, not even any bones! But my nation respects your nation. We bless it, release it, and become better beings for having passed this way. (*Mutant Message Down Under*, p. 75)

Will they ever say 'we do not judge'? How clean are their own bums? Have they ever compared bums, not to mention notes?

Martin Heidegger says,

Among the various disciplines everywhere today there are freshly awakened tendencies to put research on new foundations. (*Being and Time*, p. 29)

And the words 'new foundations' immediately put me in mind of the new Australian practices in pulling down an old house and erecting an entire new property on its old foundations to sell for more than just the old property as it is. The times they are achanging, and fast.

I see the world in ironies, in terms of ironies. Someone, don't ask me who, says to me that he wants to kill himself and feels from time to time on the edge of explosion. This is someone who has an annual income of about 150 thousand and good prospects of a promotion to a senior position in the company, compared with someone like me whose weekly income has now dropped to zero or slightly more than zero, in two digits, and who hardly ever entertains thoughts of self-killing.

A remark she said after I shared my thoughts above with her goes that the poorer you are and the more misery you suffer, the more you tend to cling to life. And it is that remark that made me realise that the meaning of something I failed to grasp in the wild grasses outside on my daily walks is this: they are at their most energetic and lively when they are unwanted, not even looked at, certainly never gathered and brought home for decoration.

In that book, one saw statues made by the Aboriginals, including one without pupils in the eyes. The Aboriginal explanation is

> You believe Divine Oneness sees and judges people… We think of Divine Oneness as feeling the intent and the emotion of beings – not as interested in what we do as why we do it. (*Mutant Message Down Under*, p. 146)

That reminds me of the blind Greek statues and that, too, reminds me of Ralph Waldo Emerson's beautification of the eye as 'the best of the artists' and 'the best composer.'[65]

His views of beauty I now find boringly narrow.

William Dunbar's 'In prais of wemen', the title alone, echoes *Dream of the Red Mansions* with its remark on women better than men in everything:

> 今风尘碌碌，一事无成，忽念及当日所有之女子，一一细考较去，觉其行止见识皆 出我之上。

Something similar attests to the devaluation of men to an animalistic level in Patrick White's *The Living and the Dead*, where, when Catherine Standish and Wally Collins are together, 'she was grateful for his presence, the mere animal presence'. (p. 270)

In the same book, I find words or lines of immense significance, such as this:

> 金满箱，银满箱，转眼乞丐人皆谤。

My translation:

Boxes of gold and boxes of silver but, in the twinkling of an eye, you are a beggar that everyone denounces.

You think that's a reference to the Chinese people only because it's written in Chinese? Think of Jeffrey Epstein.

♪♪

One character in *Dream of the Red Mansions* describes the age in which he lives as the best of the times, in Chinese terms, as '太平无为之世', literally, a world of peacefulness and doing-nothingness, doing nothing as in a Taoist sense.

Come to think of it, a world and time of no peace is often one with wanting to do something. It's that doing-somethingness collectively that makes the world chaotic.

♪♪

These words I like: 'a monopoly of disappointment' (p. 86), 'die of vexation' (p. 87), very close to the Chinese expression, *fansi le* (烦死了), 'the Ah! of things' (p. 86), and 'those dedicated to negation' (p. 87), all from Cioran's *Drawn and Quartered*.

♪♪

And then this, like a comment on my previously said:

> What a pity that 'nothingness' has been devalued by an abuse of it made by philosophers unworthy of it! (*Drawn and Quartered*, p. 86)

♪♪

In regard to the extremity of taboos, Freud says,

> The dread of uttering a dead person's name extends, indeed, to an avoidance of the mention of anything in which the dead man played a part; and an important consequence of this process of suppression is that these peoples possess no tradition and no historical memory, so that any research into their early history is faced by the greatest difficulties. (*Totem and Taboo*, pp. 55–6)

This is the first time when I coined the words 'national taboo', to describe the Chinese official suppression of anything written about the

June 4th Massacre on 4 June 1989, and anything mentioned about Xinjiang. In late 1999, when I went to Peking University as an Asialink writer in residence there, I mentioned Wei Jingsheng but a postgraduate student professed that he had never heard the name.

The philosophy of Chinese wisdoms, such as this:

一个和尚挑水吃，两个和尚抬水吃，三个和尚没水吃

Let me attempt a Google Translate translation:

One monk carried water to eat, two monks carried water to eat, three monks had no water to eat.

A minor correction by me:

One monk shoulder-poles water to eat, two monks carry water to eat and three monks have no water to eat.

This wisdom when it came to me this morning prompted me to think along the lines of poetry or poets, with the result that goes,

One poet writes poetry. Two poets talk poetry. Three poets, no poetry.

Cioran is different from me in at least one respect: he never criticises France.

Still, I like what he said here:

A self-respecting man is a man without a country. A fatherland is birdlime... (*Drawn and Quartered*, p. 89)

Not just 'birdlime', I don't think. But fatherland is a prison.

A remark on women:

I don't know anything about them women. I s'pose they're bad, but I don't suppose they're worse than men has made them.

Now that's what the Giraffe said, a character in *Send Round the Hat*.[66]

Self-interviews. Something I did years ago, in the early 1980s, late 1990s and late 2020s, either Yu interviewing Ouyang, or the other way round.

Patrick White had anticipated me by forty years. In his second novel, there is a sentence that goes, 'Muriel Raphael was deliberately making a second Muriel Raphael that overlaid the first…'[67]

And I made a mistake when trying to recall the title; I thought it was *The Living of the Dead*. A slip of the memory, and the tongue.

Among many self-related words, such as self-interviews and self-comments, both of my own coinage, and practice, I now learnt a third, from White – 'self-encouraged', as in the semi-sentence, 'their self-encouraged loves and hates'. (Ibid., p. 275)

A piece of Confucianism:

叶公语孔子曰:'吾党有直躬者,其父攘羊,而子证之。'孔子曰:'吾党之直者 异于是:父为子隐,子为父隐,直在其中矣。'

Google Translate sought:

Confucius Ye Gongyu said, 'Our party has those who bow straight, and his father threw the sheep, but the son proves it.' Confucius said, 'The straight of our party is different from this: the father is hidden by the son, the son is hidden by the father, and straight in it.'

My comment: absolutely awful translation!

The gist of this is that Ye Gong tells of an honest person who informs against his father because he has stolen a sheep while Confucius rebuts that by saying that all he knows is that when a father hides something on behalf of his son and when his son hides something on behalf of his father there is honesty in it.

I wonder what Ye Gong and Confucius's take on Prosper Mérimée's short story 'Mateo Falcone', in which the father kills his ten-year-old son because of his act of betrayal?

♪♪

We – XFYD and I – were standing outside the shopping mall and smoking, talking about a poet we both knew and that is now on no communicating terms with neither of us, one who thinks he is the best of all living Chinese poets when XFYD observed, quoting an ancient Chinese saying that goes, 文无第一，武无第二, to which I nodded my agreement.

Let me attempt a translation through Google Translate:

Wen has no first, Wu has no second.

Paraphrased, it means literature has no first, and martial arts has no second. Further paraphrased, it means that there's no one who can be rated the best of all in literature while someone must be the first and the best in martial arts, suggesting no possibility of draws in the latter and good qualities to varying degrees in the former.

♪♪

I am beginning to find Emerson boring, his prose heavy, like waters that don't flow, not attractive to someone like me who used to be thrilled with his words in my late twenties.

When he said, 'In private places, among sordid objects, an act of truth or heroism seems at once to draw to itself the sky as its temple, the sun as its candle,'[68] I said, to myself, 'Come on, this is too romantic for me. Think of Osman Shaptafaj or John Edwards. What acts of truth of theirs can draw to themselves the sky as blah blah blah?'

♪♪

Martin Heidegger: 'the history of literature is to become the history of problems'. (*Being and Time*, p. 30)

And I thought, exactly, the same way the history of shitting is to become, and has become, the history of shitting problems.

♪♪

Man: Physical exercises lead to strength and energy, in the form of semen. Ejaculated, it turns into instant trash.

Woman: That's because nothing is made for procreation. For your own pleasure, you dump it inside me.

Man starts singing, as a distraction.

♪♪

I said to him when I met AM yesterday in Castlemaine, 'I am writing a new book, intending to break all the rules, in an unpublishable fashion, following the tradition of notes-fiction that I have turned into notes-nonfiction, in fragments, at best half a page, never longer than one page, sometimes just a few words, mine invention.'

When I finished, we looked at the age-old red river gum, its trunk white, near a dry creek, in Newstead.

♪♪

'We made a boat, and we disappeared', a line by Argyris Hionis, now Chionis, a favourite Greek poet of mine that puts me strongly in mind of two lines by Su Shi: 小舟从此逝，江海寄余生, which I rendered in a book as

I wish I could disappear in my tiny little boat
And spend the rest of my life in the rivers and seas.[69]

I'll talk more about Hionis.

♪♪

O to AM: 'After the first stage of difficult publication, I have entered a higher stage of harder rejection and indifference, my single-copy editions of all my rejected work standing as tombstones of achievement, rejection, failure and defeat.'

Su Shi. Nickname, Su Dongpo. In English, Eastern Slope Su. Written into my novel *The Eastern Slope Chronicle* (2002). He wrote a prose poem, 'Ode to Pigmeat', its Chinese version below:

净洗铛，少著水，柴头罨烟焰不起。待他自熟莫催他，火候足时他自美。黄州好猪肉，价贱如泥土。贵者不肯吃，贫者不解煮，早晨起来打两碗，饱得自家君莫管。

I'll Google Translate it first:

Washing the pan, without water, can't afford to smoke. Don't urge him until he gets acquainted with himself, he is beautiful when he is warm enough. Huangzhou's good pork is as cheap as dirt. The rich refuse to eat, the poor do not decompose, so they get up in the morning and play two bowls, and they are too full to take care of them.

And Ouyang Translate it:

An Ode to Pigmeat

Wash the wok clean. Put in a bit of water. Light up the firewood. But don't let it burst into flames. Don't be in a hurry. Let it cook itself. When there is enough heat, it will be beautiful. There is good pigmeat in Huangzhou, as cheap as mud. The rich won't touch it. The poor don't know how to cook it. In the mornings I'll eat two bowls. When I am full, it's none of your business.

I now wonder if 'the rich' were Muslims.

BTW, pigmeat prepared in the Eastern Slope Su style is now famously called '东坡肉', Eastern Slope Meat, or Dongpo Rou.

He asked about Xi, wondering if he struck terror into every national of China, like Mao.

I said no. 'He is just an ordinary fellow. One doesn't have to care about him or pretend to love him. It's a different time and age now. If he wants to hold power for good, it's his own business. One doesn't care as long as the country is well run. Even though one doesn't feel good about it, one doesn't have to speak openly about it.'

♪♪

On my way to Castlemaine, I heard someone say on radio that political correctness is such one dared not even laugh any more.

I briefed him on my comparison of that with Mao's time when everyone had to quote him in all events, to say nothing of putting his words on the walls across the country, such as this one:

忙时吃干，闲时吃稀。

Google Translated as

Eat dry when you are busy, thin when you are free.

Fairly okay, as I chuckled to myself, with my own that follows:

Eat dry rice when busy and eat it thinned when not.

♪♪

It is the dry creek bed in Newstead, and the story of my billionaire poet friend, that recalled the Chinese saying, 三十年河东，三十年河西, literally, thirty years east of the river and thirty years west of the river.

Thirty years ago, I was a poor student from China. Thirty years after, C, my poet friend, is a billionaire from China, too. He bought a property for six million-plus and had five million deposited in an Australian bank as a security for his and his family's permanent residence.

Thirty years ago, China listened and followed. Thirty years after, China disobeys and says no. Thirty years east of river, now.

♪♪

'What they didn't like, they encourage others to do. No one was shocked when I read "Fuck you, Australia". Everyone laughed when I warned them that I was about to read something that might offend them. In Hong Kong, in a festival reading, I did the same thing. They were offended. One Australian poet allegedly said that such poets should not have been funded for overseas trips. You are right to say that context is everything. But what they didn't like us to do about them they encourage us to do against our own original homeland. Writers who defected from China or who are disaffected with China are encouraged to write books of fiction or nonfiction to denounce their own motherland or fatherland. How ridiculous is that?'

In my hometown Huangzhou, when I was a teenager, people didn't call people *gao*, high. They referred to them as *chang*, long.

It is not till I am more than halfway before I reached the age of sixty-six when I realised they also use the word 'long' to describe height. In 'Send round the hat',[70] the Giraffe says, 'The trouble is that I'm so long, and I always seem to get shook after little girls.' (p. 23) And he adds, 'sometimes I wish that I wasn't so blessed long'. (p. 24)

I'll quote you something and show you something else, the quote first:

> I have always been attracted by lost causes, by individuals without a hope of success, whose follies I have espoused until I suffer from them almost as much as they do. When you are committed to tormenting yourself, your own torments, however enormous, are not enough; you fling yourself on those of others as well, you appropriate them, you make yourself doubly, trebly – what am I saying? a hundredfold miserable.[71]

Something else below:

《屠宰場》

So bored! So bored! 聽音樂驅趕 boredom! 聽什麼呢?加拿大歌曲!音符一跑出錄音機，我就感到更加無聊。關掉!再換一個。鄧麗君!不行，更無聊。中國二胡曲。現在感覺怎麼樣?我搖搖頭，臉上出現極度無聊的表情。完了，完了，什麼偏方都用過了，你已經不可救藥了!還聽什麼呢?中西藥都吃過了。沒有辦法。我拚命捶桌子，我把褲腿卷到膝頭，將雙腳放到桌上，墊著兩本大字典，拚命吸煙。我用手背使勁擦腑窩，然後聞它強烈的狐臭。我喊叫，我大聲打呵欠，從最高音一直到最低音，中間隔著至少兩個八度。我在心中醞釀著仇恨，將惡毒的目光投向每一個路人，尤其是女性。我要將這心靈深處的毒汁射到她們身上，使她們受傷，永遠難忘。我看見那個身個高高、大眼圓臉，面色紅潤的姑娘，真恨不得朝她啐上一口。我想像著班上最美的一個姑娘找我辦事，我對她怒斥：「滾開吧！去找別個去，不要找老子！老子跟你有什麼關係呢？」對面床上的辛穆呻吟一聲，「啪」地將書扔在桌上，說：「哎喲，以睡 dri bor 喲(以睡眠 drive boredom)！」鄧麗君的歌聲太動聽了！她使我想起了那個黃昏，那蒙在柔軟暮色中少女的臉龐，那火熱而撩逗人的歌聲，我的心跳，不知不覺地停下，卻又惶恐不安。這時什麼也無法趕走我胸中的鬱悶和無聊，還是鄧麗君的歌曲。他們(懷柔和辛穆)也在如饑似渴地聽著。懷柔睡不著爬起來一面寫日記，一面聽音樂。而辛穆陶醉在音樂中，正沉沉睡去，尋求他的好夢。我的心哭著想起工廠那冷冰冰空蕩蕩的房。小陳給我講著他的夢。「我在夢中見到最美的景色，有時有大片鮮花，白天鵝成群成群地在湖上飛來飛去。有時我獨自一人徜徉在金碧輝煌的大廳。」啊，那可憐的人！他永遠在做夢，帳子從來沒洗，黑得像抹布，破了幾個大洞。一床被子跟眼前的他，也是一蓋就是一年至兩年不定。為什麼我一生所接觸的都是這樣的人？孤兒、失去母親的人、失去父親的人、在愛情上永遠得不到滿足的人，為什麼，啊，為什麼？我的心顫抖著，痙攣著，我想大哭，我的眼睛睜得大大，等著泉水般上湧的淚水，我要把它們像自來水，不，像瀑布一樣傾瀉出去，洗乾淨他的被子，洗去這人世間的汙穢。他說，他要聽悲傷的音樂。快，快拿最傷悲的曲子，我這冷漠石頭一樣的心需要悲傷的大錘猛擊，將它擊得粉碎，讓它中心的鮮血再一次迸流，像年輕時，青春旺盛時那樣。我需要愁苦的大刀狠狠砍我，直到我遍體鱗傷。我多想出去，到那翠綠的山谷，在啼聲像鋼珠一樣亮脆的鳥叫聲和繽紛得像晚霞一樣的湖岸旁，脫得光光，跳進清澈見底的湖水中，痛痛快快，像一條魚一樣游泳起來，我憎惡世界的一切，這窒息得人透不過氣來的人屾，這純潔得像蒸餾水一樣的人間地獄。可惡！虛偽！正人君子的大笑！法律殘酷的刑具！我憎惡，我憎惡。把我捆起來，關進黑屋子，照我沒頭沒腦地用粗棒子打吧。我不怕，打死我吧！這人世是一個殘酷的屠宰場，可怕至極！

(2018 年 11 月 4 日星期天 8.41 a.m., at room 308, hbl, suibe, 拾得自我的长篇小说《绿色》第二卷)

This remark, made in *Mutant Message Down Under*, is worth quoting:

> …they [the Aborigines] don't believe ownership of land was ever intended. Land belongs to all things. Agreements and sharing are the real human way. Possession is the extreme of excluding others for self-indulgence. Before the British came, no one in Australia was without land. (p. 151)

And before that, the word 'dreamtime' is mentioned which, in my creative mind, was instantly re-coined as 'beingtime.'

Wife to Bacchus, take the sky as your dowry, be seen there
As a star…'[72]

Loved this.

'The gods take stone
And turn it into men and women;
Men and women take gods
And turn them into stone.'[73]

Loved this, too.

Black money.

My self-shame is deepened whenever not even moneyed Chinese have respect as their moneyed Western counterparts command because if they have money they must have got it by dirty means. In a word, black money.

I thought of A's comment on all international wars based on one thing: trade. Two wars with China over opium. (See, for example, https://www.bbc.com/news/world-asia-india-49404024)

Even though it's hard to find exactly how much money Great Britain made from its two opium wars with China, one source says that ten years after the First Opium War, China lost its silver externally, to the amount of 150 million taels. (See https://baike.baidu.com/item/鸦片贸易)

Wasn't that black money made by the others, mainly the Brits?

Another outburst, by this ordinary man, in the presence of his best friend and his wife:

> With those tombstones of books, I'll say no to all those who have rejected me, not allowing them to publish anything of mine for a decade, no, for a century at least, when all the people who know me are dead, when I am dead, and when only the living can somehow find access to my single-copy books.

His wife talked about him being described by someone I really dislike because he once made the mistake of referring to my collection *The Kingsbury Tales: A Novel* as written by Roberto Bolano, refusing to make the correction after I emailed him about it.

She said, 'He referred to him as having "steely eyes" –'

I laughed as I looked to check if they were really 'steely' when he made himself cross-eyed.

I laughed even harder when I saw that and saw the absurdity of the word 'steely'.

I got an email in the morning but because I was busy writing I had to wait till this arvo to write a reply.

Not long afterwards, I got an email, a semi-found poem without the quotation marks:

Laughing a Failure Poem

The tea of loose leaves
The purple fig of colour
Sweet as honey
I ate it avidly
Watched over
By my God of Balance

My immediate response:

Good on u and the poem but I wanted the fig of colour in as that indicates my status: a person of colour or commonly known as 'POC', worse than a POW.

What I then did is I wrote a poem and emailed it to him, with these words in the subject: 'A poem in return for the missing fig':

This is

A fig of colour
A fish of colour
A fetish of colour

A rain of colour
A rain bow of colour
A ruin of colour

A bowl of colour
A bullet of colour
A bomb of colour

A flower of colour
A flow of colour
A fake of colour

A cloud of colour
A covid-19 of colour
A con, corn, of colour

A blade of grass of colur
A breath of colour
A breach of colour

A vaccsin of colour
A vast majority of colour
A victory of colour

A colour of no colour
A colour of没colour
A colour of殁colour

(4.03 p.m., Sunday 11/4/2021, at home in K) (from my《无事记》, 第 21 卷)

I'll talk more about my God of Balance when I have time.

This is what I wrote and emailed him, just now, with 'I'm going to submit' in the subject:

The novel to 3,000 publishers around the world and wait for the demise. Then I'll publish a single copy. Books are not meant for money; they are spirits that carry far and wide and long and high. And for all eternity you only need one zhiyin or zhixin, or both.

Over breakfast, I said to her, 'If you have your work translated into Russian, it's like into another China. No payments. No permissions sought. No updates. The only benefit: you get a name in Russia and Russian.'

I was referring to my findings this morning about a website that features an interview with me by Amelia Dale, in English, now in Russian: https://versevagrant.com/2018/07/28/неустанноедвижение-вниз-интервью-с-о/

Am translating a poem, by Xifeng Yedu, these three lines just done:

偌大酒店似乎只我一名住客
被自由所因者，足以操死
一头牛，……

    And my translation:

The huge hotel seemed to have me alone, the single guest
Those imprisoned by freedom are enough to fuck a cow
Dead,…

Did someone say 'Reversal is the way of the Tao'? Or the other way round, 'The way of the Tao is reversal'?

    Either way, it's the same. The Chinese way of thinking is exactly the opposite of the Western way of thinking.

    I have no examples to offer. Check my *Flag of Permanent Defeat* (2019). Enough said, poetically. Or my 《译心雕虫》(2013)。

I did something imperceptibly yesterday. I removed one posting each of my published poem in *Quadrant* (March 2021), received yesterday afternoon, respectively at FB and Instagram as I realised that by doing so I may have offended some sensibilities.

    But, going through the magazine at night, I found it interestingly reactionary, such as this remark on p. 55 that goes, 'Indigenous literature (like much New Age white literature, if we must now speak in these racial terms) seems more like therapy than literature.'

    And something quoted by Ross Terrill, of a letter from Beijing declining to grant entry to Pearl S. Buck to China to attend the Mao–Nixon summit in 1972 because her works expressed 'an attitude of distorting, smear, and vilification towards the people of new China and its leaders', p. 83, caught my attention, a quintessential example of the reversal of the Tao: what you like, so much so that she got the Nobel prize in lit, is what they hate, echoing Mao's words, 'We are against whatever our enemy is for and for whatever our enemy is against.'

When he said this, 'My dear friend, I'm becoming more and more solitary,' my interest was aroused and when he said further, 'Anything and everything is capable of provoking me,'[74] I thought I would have twenty years ago. But not any more.

No one says it better of the human nature loving praises and hating criticisms than Ovid, almost Covid, when he says this,

> When it's praised, then Juno's peacock displays its plumage;
> If you stare without comment – no show.
> Even racehorses, back in the paddock, respond with pleasure
> To a combed mane, a pat on the neck.[75]

In the final analysis, human beings are animals. They are capable of thinking, most times of money.

My response to Emerson's epigram that 'Nothing divine dies. All good is eternally reproductive', (p. 25) is 'All bad, too!'

I like *The Getting of Wisdom* by Henry Handel Richardson. Like 'Henry' that she lied about, her character Laura makes the discovery about the pleasure of lying in that 'as soon as you put pen to paper, provided you kept one foot planted on probability, you might lie as hard as you liked: indeed, the more vigorously you lied, the louder would be your hearers' applause.'[76]

Something to share about how I wrote my novel 《淘金地》. I produced two to three thousand characters daily, starting from a total blankness in my mind when things happened, one Chinese word after another, till the pages were filled, the way Ted Hughes did his poem 'The Thought Fox'.

The 'wounded ringdove' (*Drawn and Quartered*, p. 96) recalls a similar incident I had a few weeks ago in the city of Melbourne where, in a street corner, I saw a black bird perched underneath a chair without trying to get away from me as I got near it, raising its eyes towards me in a timid but bold way. It's not till then that I realised it might have somehow got wounded. The thought came to me to get it in my hands, put it in my bag and go home by tram with it. But where would I keep it? How can I keep it alive? What can I feed it? What if it died on the way? It's all these imagined consequences that stopped me from doing anything but let it go. When I came back half an hour later, it's nowhere to be found.

> 'To have the sense of the *perpetual* only in the negative, in what does harm, in what thwarts being. Perpetuity of threat, of frustration, of longed-for and failed ecstasy, of an absolute glimpsed and rarely achieved; yet sometimes transcended, skipped over, as when you escape God…' (*Drawn and Quartered*, p. 96)

Exactly how I have been feeling lately.

In Cathay, according to what's recorded in *The Travels of Marco Polo*,

> They hold that as soon as a man is dead he enters into another body; and according as he has conducted himself well or ill in life, he passes from good to better or from bad to worse. That is to say, if he is a man of humble rank and has behaved well and virtuously in life, he will be reborn after death from a gentlewoman and will be a gentleman, and thereafter from the womb of a noblewoman and will become a nobleman; and so he follows an ever upward path culminating in assumption into the Deity. But, if he is a man of good birth and has behaved badly, he will be reborn as the son of a peasant; from a peasant's life he will pass to a dog's and so continually downwards.[77]

Now, that's God of Balance at work, again.

You want an example of the aforementioned reversal? Here you are, with something I've just translated from the Chinese, with the Chinese version placed ahead of the translation:

文学奖视野下的当代台湾散文观察

刘秀珍

摘要：当代台湾散文的发展脉络与各类文学奖的设立与变迁密切相关。从上世纪五六十年代的抒情文体定位，到九十年代末地方文学奖推动新乡土散文兴起，乃至 21 世纪以来文学奖被诟病为散文虚构盛行的推手与"试炼人心"的竞技场，并由此引发持续争议，从中可窥见台湾散文与文学奖之间错综复杂的生态关系。

关键词：文学奖；台湾散文；散文虚构

An Observation of Contemporary Taiwanese Prose in the Perspective of Literary Awards

Liu Xiuzhen

Abstract:

Veins of development of contemporary Taiwanese prose are closely associated with the set-up and changes of various categories of literary awards. One can gain glimpses into the complex ecological relationships between Taiwanese prose and literary awards from what happened in the positioning of the lyrical genre in the 1950s and 1960s, to the end of 1990s when local literary awards led to the rise of new native prose until the 21st century and since when literary awards were critiqued as a force pushing for the prosperity of prose fiction and an arena for 'testing the human heart'.

Keywords: Literary awards, Taiwanese prose, prose fiction

Note that the English translation, particularly of the second sentence, works from the end of the Chinese sentence backwards.

The rest of it is only meant for the understanding.

♪♪

I think the word should be 'negative', not 'positive', if you read the following quote:

> [General Blamey] was nothing if not positive: he seldom spared anybody's feelings, and so he became a controversial figure. He had plenty of critics, and not a few detractors.[78]

There being no one to discuss this with, I include it here for myself.

♪♪

We've stopped watching any TV after the daily news on SBS. What do we watch? We watch small videos on FB, such as this one we bumped into tonight: https://fb.watch/4SqQEGwFKr/, something very real that happened on 5/1/2021 in Beijing when the public security came in to forcibly dismantle the local buildings despite the police woman's feeble attempts to stop them.

♪♪

The appearance of a Chinese in an Australian fiction, any Australian fiction for that matter, written by the whites, has to be necessarily described with words such as 'ugly'. See this I've just come across:

> 'You mind your own business.' Cindie spoke with asperity, but as she turned and looked full into the Celestial's broad ugly face, she was unable to refrain from emulating his grin.[79]

The 'Celestial's name is Lo How. I wonder how he would have described Cindie.

♪♪

Shit is delightful to write about and to shit, without a glitch. Refer to the first chapter, respectively, of Mo Yan's *Red Locust* and Yu Hua's *Brothers*, each saturated with shit.

And refer, too, to Alexander Solzhenitshyn's *The Gulag Archipelago*, where, on p. 23, the guards tell the prisoners to shit fast, saying that

'With us, they do it quickly!', to which one of the prisoners replies, 'And with us we do it slowly,'…

When shit like that happens, it's often unforgettable.

I thought I wrote something a few days ago professing that I no longer love. Today, I saw this:

One does not die of love unrequited but of ceasing to love.'80

Just what I want.

A loser, a hater of oneself for being a loser, a liker of the loser status, a time waster, a poetry writer, a lover, a loser of love.

Is that me in a nutshell?

Decided not to watch TV over breakfast. Overload of news. One gets the same thing variously, repeatedly, till one gets numb.

Then, a voice came back from a conference dinner: 'My husband and I, in Denmark. Owned only a black and white TV. Hardly ever watched it. Natural sounds were infinitely better.'

Must have been in or around 2000 when you went to a conference in Guangzhou after you did the one in Taiwan, memory suggested.

Sixty-five thousand dollars for the two top winners and 10,000 dollars for each shortlisted. That's how much poetry is worth. I get it. The rest of them get nothing. They wasted their money in submitting a number of free copies et cetera.

'It's pure luck,' said A.

'It's pure chance at work,' said O.

I saw the dead body of a bird this morning. And read a couple of poems about death. Pure chance.

🎵

The real writer writes about beings, things, events, he does not write about writing, he uses words but does not linger over them, making them the object of his ruminations. He will be anything and everything except an anatomist of the Word. Dissecting of language is the fad of those who, having nothing to say, confine themselves to the saying. (*Drawn and Quartered*, pp. 100–101)

My comment: yes and no.

🎵

Someone said something decades ago to this effect that China is a shadow of the West, its people shadows of Western people.

I'm translating abstracts and keywords of academic articles for the new issue of *Huawen wenxue*. Hereby I confirm that view by saying that these writers can't think without quoting Western theorists, such as Henri Lefebvre, another French person whose name I can't put down correctly multiple times and whose theory I have not read, won't bother reading perhaps for the rest of my life.

Don't think I can allow *my* mind to be part of *his* produced space.

🎵

《随译集》。

Typeset in hand now. Proofreading. Delighted with this:

I don't take life very seriously. It's hard to get into this world and hard to get out of it. And what's in between doesn't make much sense. If that sounds pessimistic, let it stand.[81]

BTW, it's my 130th book and one possible translation of the title would be *Translated, Randomly*. Scheduled number of copies at publication: 10.

🎵

Just now, bumped into this, quoted of Nieztcher – let me check, oh, Nietzsche – that goes, 'Some men are born posthumously.'

Refer to my new book, 《随译集》, being proofread, p. 49.

This morning, while I was walking in the park, I thought of something and texted it to the person in question again:

> Basically, I always think that is unjust and unfair although I'm prepared to forgive and forget

BTW, I said to myself, you wrote seven poems this morning, outside on your walk.

I'll write something here, then text it to her, to remind her:

> I wrote an email to you days ago to purchase a few copies of my *Living After Death*. But haven't heard back. Hope you are well.

A poem I wrote, while taking shit for a third time; the second time nothing came out:

A Comment

The whites are predatory
But they like what they love
They love what they like

And they make money

Yu wrote to Ouyang,

> They want to monopolise everything, politically, economically, financially, religiously, and now, they want to monopolise the moral high ground by owning the PC.
>
> Who are 'They', anyway?

♪♪

Ouyang to Yu,

> I've just 'Unfollowed' a publisher who has recently rejected my novel, a white person, and did not bother replying to my request for the deletion of my manuscript from their file, so unprofessional.

♪♪

Pointedly, I noticed something that goes,

> People who are always up in arms about things are the greatest bores in the world.[82]

   It's Cupid who said that to Laura.

I always wanted to write about bad teeth because I had bad teeth. I have never come across writings about bad teeth. But in this novel, I did: 'extravagantly long hair, bad teeth and…'[83] (p. 75) and 'Suddenly she smiled, and despite the bad teeth she became almost attractive.' (p. 76)

   I think, in a strange way, good literature has got to be associated with bad teeth, bad smells and generally bad things. Not PC. Once PCed, literature is dead.

Man 'is placed in the centre of beings, and a ray of relation passes from every other being to him.'[84]

   Really? American 'man' did you mean? Not woman? Not to her?

   I am finding Emerson harder going than before, my interest waning.

On the other hand, Emerson's quoted 'voice of Paul, who calls the human corpses a seed – "It is sown a natural body; it is raised a spiritual body,"' – is what I like.

♪♭♪

Bought a copy of *Life's Little Ironies* by Thomas Hardy and came across this remark about

> the belief of the British parent that a bad marriage with its aversions is better than free womanhood with its interests, dignity, and leisure…[85]

And I thought of the current Chinese recommendation to marriageable women: 干得好不如嫁得好 (roughly, to be well married is better than to be well achieved).

♪♭♪

Don't ask me who said this but he said that Australia is

> a hateful country, and I think if I were 15 years younger I would go away and stay away for good.[86]

And that reminds of a poem titled 'Fuck you, Australia'[87] that has found its way into a Denmark-based textbook for secondary schools in Denmark.

♪♭♪

'But they both liked to watch bad television once a week.'[88] Don't worry about who said it. My wife and I don't even watch TV any more except the news. Otherwise, we watch small video clips on FB, on a nightly basis. Very bad 'TV', but infinitely more interesting than any 'bad television'. The following three items are what we've just watched together:

1. https://fb.watch/4Wmv22Y eIl/
2. https://fb.watch/4Wn606R8XP/

♪♭♪

Nothing is good enough. One always seeks alternatives. For Marlo Morgan, she found it in the Aboriginal culture, as a possible solution to American problems:

> I thought of people at home in the United States: the number of

young people who seemed to have no sense of direction or purpose, the homeless people who think they have nothing to offer society, the addicted individuals who want to function in some reality other than the one we are in. I wished I could bring them here, to witness how little it takes, sometimes, to be a benefit to your community, and how wonderful it is to know and experience a sense of self-worth.[89]

I wish, too.

The most interesting revelation came when she was accepted by the Aboriginal community and was named by them 'Two Hearts'. (p. 166)

Remember what the title of my third poetry collection in Australia is? *Two Hearts, Two Tongues and Rain-coloured Eyes*. (Wild Peony, 2002)

A negative comment on Hamlet by a woman here:

> ...after all, what is he? What is he but vicious, maudlin, spiteful, and sensitive to nothing but his own headaches? I find him completely unprepossessing.[90]

I corrected a typo just now, turning 'home' back into 'hope', the two not interchangeable anyway but the latter probably a more problematic condition than the former or else Cioran would not have made the remark that goes,

> One is and remains a slave as long as one is not cured of hoping. (*Drawn and Quartered*, p. 102)

A friend of mine, from country D, has his email address containing the word 'hopeless'.

Grammatical problems are everything because my eyes see them everywhere, such as in *The Good Soldier* by Ford Madox Ford, with this: 'and I pray God that he is really at peace,...'[91] (p. 54)

Connie Tiarks is an awkward character, to say the least, and White is quite unfair in making her so. Still, she resembles Jing in *The English Class* (2010) in that she 'wrote mentally' (*The Living and the Dead*, p. 282) whereas Jing is a head-writer.

I like the sentence 'The question of existence is one of Dasein's ontical "affairs"' (*Being and Time*, p. 33) as it is mildly reminiscent of Heidegger's own affairs.

About eight years ago, a new law was introduced in China that children must visit their parents or face fines or jail terms.

    It's nothing new because in *The Travels of Marco Polo*, it is observed,

> They treat their father and mother with profound respect. If it should happen that a child does anything to displease his parents or fails to remember them in their need, there is a department of state whose sole function it is to impose severe penalties on those who are found guilty of such ingratitude.[92]

An instance of balance:

> The world has long ago settled that morality and virtue are what bring men peace at the last. 'Be virtuous,' says the copy-book, 'and you will be happy.' Surely if a reputed virtue fails often in this respect it is only an insidious form of view, and if a reputed vice brings no very serious mischief on a man's later years it is not so bad a vice as it is said to be.[93]

>   Now should I complain,
>   or warn you,
> That no one now distinguishes right from wrong?[94]

I thought it was about now. But it's only Ovid about his own time.

'The History of Our Sewage Disposal System', the title of chapter 2 in Solzhenitsyn's *The Gulag Archipelago* (p. 24), induced something similar to the future title of a book I could write: *The History of a Poet's Shit*.

I guess I could add the word 'living' to the word 'poet'.

I have always been labouring under the illusion that I'm at odds with the rest of the world as they are with me till I heard what he said:

> I do not struggle against the world, I struggle against a greater force, against my weariness of the world. (*Drawn and Quartered*, p. 105)

Today. The second day of my first arrival in Australia thirty years ago. I made a mistake. In reading a passage in Freud's *Time and Being* – no, I mean *Totem and Taboo* – I thought I saw 'hackground' when I saw 'background'. And I decided to keep it.

Please refer to the handwritten one on p. 63 of my copy.

More geese than swans now live, more fools than wise.[95]

The last line in the poem 'The Silver Swan'.

Did they know that the Chinese refer to the swans as 天鹅? Literally, sky geese. Or heaven geese.

I love 《增广贤文》, one of the sayings in which goes, '人一走，茶就凉' ('The second you leave, the tea goes cold.'), the other one being, '人情似纸张张薄，世事如棋局局新。' ("The human relationship is as thin as a piece of paper the same way each chess game is new when played.')[96]

♪♪

Allow me to keep making mistakes. Another one this morning: Hollowcaused.

♪♪

Finished reading *Mutant Message Down Under* and checked its hackground information when, for the first time, I learnt that the author publicly confessed she had faked it.

That's when I felt, as a Chinese saying goes, like having swallowed a fly.

♪♪

增广贤文 (7)
我喜欢里面这句话：'众星朗朗，不如孤月独明'。随译如下：

Not even the cluster of bright stars can match the solitary light of a lonely moon.

随译完后，我听见自己说: Isn't that wonderful?[97]

♪♪

《火力点》(1)
这是我自 2011 年以来，写的一首二行体长诗。前不久，我开始一天三段或六段或最多九段，把它放到我的双语网站上 (https:// youyang2.blogspot.com)，今天又顺次选了 3 段放上 去，忽然觉得，这三段好像很值得随译一下，就随意了，随译了，就直接放在下面吧，读者可以自己选择对照：

435.
你死了后　就不可能再死了
(12.2.3 夜)

436.
我不用爬山，我的脑比山高
我不用下海，我的脑比海深
(12.2.3)

437.
这边的土地一抓满手是血

因为它充满了仇恨

随译如下：

435.
When you die
You can't die again
(2020.5.23 晨译)

436.
I don't need to climb the mountains, my brain higher than them
I don't need to go down the sea, my brain deeper than the sea
(2020.5.23 晨译)

437.
You take a grab of the earth here and your hand is smeared with blood

Because it is filled with hatred

(2020.5.23 晨译)[98]

♪♪

Just now, a thought came to me, in this voice:

> Dear D-, this is the book you wanted me to write about you. Here it is, delivered from hell, after my death, and published by Death Inc. Unlimited, with all my love and more.

Right, I thought. That could serve as the beginning of my next novel. Not yet titled.

♪♪

Mention.

On p. 356, he mentions 'prime minister Harold Holt.' On p. 357, he mentions 'the immigration minister, Bill Snedden.' But, on the same page, 357, when he says, 'A Chinese Australian was elected president of the Northern Territory Assembly in 1965 and the following year made mayor of Darwin,' he doesn't mention the name.[99]

How snobbish is that?

♪♪

I laughed when I saw PM John Gorton's promise to an audience in Singapore in 1971 that 'Australia would soon display a "complete lack of consciousness of difference between the races"',[100] and reminded myself of an article I read this morning, titled, 'More allegations of racism from former Neighbours actors' (https://www.abc.net.au/news/2021-04-19/more-allegations-of-racism-from-former-neighbours-actors/100078186).

That's a gap of fifty years and nothing much has changed at all.

♪♪

'[T]he Australian defeat in Vietnam.' (Day, p. 358) At the sight of these five words, my reaction is like: when did Australia ever win when assisting the English aggressors and American invaders? Have they ever won a just war?

♪♪

'John Ivy'.[101] A name I could keep in mind for future creation.

See this sentence:

Ella Marchmill had often and often scanned the rival poet's work…[102]

That 'often and often' is evocative of the Chinese double-word 'changchang': 常常, literally, often-often.

Valerie, in choosing who to invite to her wedding, decides she 'really hated her. But she would have to be asked.'[103]

I like that.

After Virginia runs Hamlet down, Pete, her lover, runs her down to her face, saying to her, among other things, 'In other less charitable company you would have had your balls chopped off.'[104]

I laughed, and wondered, did Virginia have 'balls'?

White must be one of the weirdest literary weirdos I've ever encountered. Just read these:

> …there were the priests as white as aspirin…you put up a hand to hide your own bones and a transparent, fruitless egg.[105]

No, I mean, he really is a most poetic novelist, particularly with this book, *TLATD*.

In the middle of translating a poem by XFYD, I received an email letter of rejection and I wrote an immediate reply,

> Hi C-,
> I'm made uncomfortable by your constant reference to me as someone based in Victoria as a reason for exclusion. I'm based in Victoria, but I came from China and am an Australian citizen. It is true that SLV has collected my material. It it true, too, that they haven't collected this material I'm offering nor are they continuing to collect everything I wrote.
> Honestly, I don't care whether you collect my published material or not. That's not even collectible. But I detest your excuses. I am based in Australia. I am an Australian author. I offer my mate-

rial to you now. If you knock it back. Fine. I won't be offering again. But your reasons for exclusion are so boring and disgusting.
Cheers

Acquaintance? What a boring word! What about acquainstance? Or a-quaint-antce? No, all boring. See its Chinese equivalent in my translation: a cooked person.

Lesson learnt: it's always a good idea to speak or think outside Englishit.

My comment on almost four pages of taunting administered by Pete to Ginny is two words handwritten on p. 89 of *The Dwarfs* by Pinter: 'Tyranny' and 'Boring.'

White is good at saying things half-finished. One instance: '...the eyes half-doze, half-flicker, that wondered if the telephone.'[106]

I like what I read here, enough to quote it:

> Blokes like Ayler and Coltrane and Coleman, they've been freed, man, but they're still alienated. So they've dropped the hope bit. Their music is total alienation: and as such they're the most perfect expression of our age.[107]

Sexuality. A recent poetry competition featuring the theme of *xing'ai* (sexuality or erotic love) in China was aborted because only one poet submitted his sex poem.

My open comment on that goes, to this effect: thinkable, not doable. Doable, not writeable. Writeable, not publishable.

As I spoke to A about, I'll find erotic poems I translated of Feng Menglong in the Ming dynasty. I might instead quote Cioran in tandem here:

This old sexuality is *something*, all the same… Ever since life has been life, we were right, it must be said, to make so much of it. How else account for the fact that we grow tired of everything, except of it? The oldest exercise of the living cannot fail to mark us, and we realize that he who has no dealing with it is a being apart – an outcast or a saint. (*Drawn and Quartered*, p. 104)

Last night at Franko's place. He said, 'Have you finished your book?' I said, 'Which one?' Fact is, I revealed I was writing a number of books at the same time.

How close the Chinese and the Irish can be when Sax Rohmer, an Irishman, creates Fu Manchu, a Chinese man, 'stark raving mad, or the Saviour of the Indian Empire – perhaps of all Western civilization'?[108]

And a 434-pager, of A4 size, priced at $1 only. So Chinesely cheap.

Bell and Road deal with China cancelled today (see: https://fortune.com/2021/04/22/china-australia-belt-and-road-infrastructure-deal-cancel/).

And I happened to read this, also today, that

> Some [Australians] had also been pressed into service to fight a feared Chinese foe only to watch Australian wheat farmers sell their harvests in Beijing and their American ally establish relations with China in 1972 without consulting or informing Australia. (David Day, pp. 364–5)

What a hilarioustory!

And it's full of mistakes, the uncorrectible kind, in fiction and outside it. Read this below, from Cindie, a comment by Aboriginal woman Minnie on a young Kanaka:

'He my husband… He make damn good music.'

The response from Cindie:

'What!' Cindie was scandalized. 'Your husband! He's only a boy!'

Followed by this:

'He old enough,' said Minnie, tersely.

The conclusion: Cindie thought of her as 'The old beast!' and that 'She would take jolly good care to keep her at a distance in the future.' (*Jean Devanny*, p. 48)

And it's history's turn to keep her, Cindie, at a distance now.

Why bother writing a book if some of it is going to be thought of as wrong in the future?

Two lines by Kenneth Koch that capture the spirit of movement towards freedom:

The opening up of freedom takes place in steps:
First one speaks of the ocean, then of the boats, then of the people on the boats, lastly of their ideas. (p. 517)

A bit simplistic but.

An ancient Chinese story in a nutshell.

The wife has an affair. She intends to poison her husband in a cup of wine. She wants the concubine to serve it on his return. The concubine, to protect him, knocks the cup on purpose. The husband, the master of the house, is so furious that he gives her a beating.

The moral of this? She suffers because of her loyalty. Hence the need to lie, to be fraudulent, in order to win trust.[109]

A friend's dad passed away. After expressing my 'deepest condolences', he answered my query, saying that it was a heart attack that finished him off at eighty-four. Following was what I said:

I see. Thank you for that. There's a Chinese expression that goes: 七十三，八十四，阎王不请自己去, meaning 73 or 84 is the most critical age. True, when this happens, there is little one can do. The Google Translate, though, doesn't work properly. The expression literally means, in my translation: at 73 or 84, you go yourself even if the Devil doesn't invite you.

Google Translate's version:

Seventy-three, eighty-four, Hades don't invite himself to go.

In eight years, I shall be reaching that critical point.

♪♪

'That's what love is: repeated sentences.'[110]

And that's what I like, recalling infinite instances of it.

♪♪

Su Shi talks about writing a postscript to a book, feeling '酒气勃勃，从指端出也'.[111]

Airs of liquor surging out of the fingertips.

♪♪

《前赤壁赋》, or 'My First Visit to the Red Cliff', by Su Shi, is one of his best-known *fu*, or, in my translation, fugue.

But, according to him, he hardly ever showed it to anyone except one or two. In his own words, '未尝轻出以示人，见者盖一二人也。'[112]

♪♪

鼻酸。 Literally, a sour nose. But I can't translate it; I simply make do. Here's an example, from my translation of Xifeng Yedu's poem, partly about his daughter:

When I saw how reluctant she was
In saying goodbye to the other kids
And in taking farewell from her teachers
She choked up as did I
Her eyes reddened as did my eyes
And if she wept, I would weep, too

But can we equate 'choke up' with 'sour nose'? I have no one to consult. All I know is that, as a Chinese person, I know how it feels to be *bisuan* (鼻酸、nose sour or a sour nose), a sharp sourness in the nose in the lead-up to surging tears or the feeling of it.

♪♪

I like what Su Shi says about dreams when he says that he's in Huangzhou where he dreams he is on the West Lake: '梦中亦知其为梦也',[113] meaning 'knowing in my dream that it is also a dream.'

Huangzhou, my hometown where I was born and grew up, got married and had our child.

♪♪

If Itchy Feet is a nickname for one who's 'always changing his job',[114] there, disappointingly, is no match for the Chinese expression 手痒, itchy hands, a reference to eagerness to take part in things, to give it a go, to say nothing of another expression: 屁眼痒, itchy bums, a Wuhan reference to police, based on a homonym.

♪♪

Just WeChatted the following to my publisher:

> writing a book of creative non-fiction, or, in my own coinage, pen-notes non-fiction (笔记非小说), in fragments, aiming at 50,000 words, a small volume. could go on for more volumes. done 31,985 words, about to wrap up shortly. Would this be something worth considering?

♪♪

After I told her about the itchy hands, my wife said, 'But it is also a description of kids who make a mess with things when their hands get itchy.'

♪♪

'Let's shed the humanities!'

I turned my head back. There was no one. Only a bird, an Australian national.

♪♪♪

Sunday morning. Translating Xifeng Yedu's poetry first thing. These four lines of a poem titled 'Caring about Dignity Only':

格里菲斯天文台
和盖蒂艺术中心
都是牛逼的地方
而且都不要钱

And my translation:

Griffith Observatory
And Getty Arts Center
Are places of *niubi* or cow pushy
And nothing is charged for admission

No explanation intended and that's the beauty of it. You either understand or you don't.

♪♪♪

Ellipsis in three dots: …
That translates into Chinese, in 6 dots: ……
To me, being means nothing. But this says it all.

♪♪♪

What later had major influence had little impact when first published, such as BAT (*Being and Time*) or not even published before the author died, such as TWOAF (*The Way of All Flesh*). And history first forgets those who win awards as soon as they are published, leaving posterity to posterity.

My novel, with only one copy published, was originally titled AODTF. Why would I tell you what it stands for?

♪♪♪

I thought of something when I saw this. I didn't make an utterance of it knowing what it was. Here you go:

Hard thorns are all that's left of the blown rose.[115]

The good that is evil. The bad that is good. That's my conclusion reached when I read him, with this:

> I have less and less discernment as to what is good and what evil. When I make no distinction whatever between the two, supposing I reach this point some day – what a step forward! Towards what? (*Drawn and Quartered*, p. 110)

Driving while listening to soldiers talking about how they felt after Afghanistan. Rage. Restless. Suicides. Boozing. Divorcing. On a sudden, a connection emerged by itself: fighting in a foreign country and migrating to one, are traumatic experiences in themselves. Loss after loss, roots removed, anger, disappointment, angst, postmigration depression, rejection, rejection and more rejection. Now, read this:

> These fits of rage, this need to explode, to spit in everyone's face, to slap one universe after the next – how to vanquish them? It would take a little turn in a cemetery, or better still, a definitive turn...[116]

Sundays for the Rest of My Life.

A title for my next novel, inspired by a thought that lately and regularly visits me: every day now feels like a Sunday to me, and that, in particular, visited me today, a Monday.

As if to provide my previous comment with a background, I heard my own comment in Chinese after reading a poetry book:

他的东西说好不好，说坏不坏，太平淡了。(His stuff is neither good nor bad. Just flat.)

Hence my addition to the either good or bad thing, with both good and bad as well as neither good nor bad.

♪♪

According to the rich poet, he had submitted his poetry to more than two hundred magazines and got only one reply at one stage in his life. Afterwards, he became a billionaire.

I said to my wife, 'If he had been successful with poetry, getting published everywhere, he would never have been so rich as he is now.'

♪♪

Chloé Zhao's remark about China being 'a place where there are lies everywhere' (https://zh.wikipedia.org/wiki/趙婷) recalls Lin Biao's words:

不说假话，办不成大事. (You can't achieve anything great without saying fake words.)

Fake words or 假话 are not exactly lies.

♪♪

Note this, only two words, by Sir Gregory Hale: 'Yellow…rising.'[117]

♪♪

Managed to finish reading a strange book that ends on an even stranger albeit poetic sentence:

They got on with the vernacular of the night.[118]

♪♪

The absurdity of English is that when I think it should be 'on', it is 'in' that is used, such as this:

He took off his glasses and placed them in his lap.[119]

It's Lawson's insistent voice that says,

The Australian Bushman is born with a mate who sticks to him through life – like a mole. They may be hundreds of miles apart sometimes, and separated for years, yet they are mates for life.

After thirty years in the country, I confess I don't know about that. My situation is more like Cioran's 'vacuum' as he defines it:

> How can you know if you are in the truth? The criterion is simple enough: if others make a vacuum around you, there is not a doubt in the world that you are closer to the essential than they. (*Drawn and Quartered*, p. 112)

And, a few days after, when I resumed reading the book, I saw this, on the same page:

> the straightest chap that ever lived – 'a white man!' (Lawson, p. 51)

Oh, I see.

Despite the fact that 'Kelvinator' is used as a nickname to refer to a woman with 'frigid air',[121] it's the brand of the first refrigerator that I bought in a garage sale, for fifty bucks, in my first year in Melbourne thirty years ago and sold for the same price a few months after.

It used to be China-bashing and now it's Australia's turn to be bashed. Just read this today (28/4/2021): https://mp.weixin.qq.com/s/CgMcs6_QPpX0lizvmB3rYw

Some of the choicest expressions for Australia include '这个国家的流氓本性' (the hooliganism of this country), '骨子里仍然是罪犯基因' (the criminal gene still in their bones), '澳大利亚这个国家实际上比无赖还无赖，比毒蛇还恶毒' (the nation of Australia is more rascal than rascals and more poisonous snakes than poisonous snakes).

He was a pure-blooded Don horse with not a drop of foreign blood in his veins…[122]

To this day, I, too, am 'a pure-blooded' Chinese. But how am I sure I'm pure? And what is the importance of purity in this day and age when identity seems to be multiply mixed?

♪♭♪

Freud sounds so arbitrary when he says, 'in some languages the words for "conscience" and "conscious" can scarcely be distinguished'. (*Totem and Taboo*, p. 68)

Did he know Chinese? Did he know that in that language it's 良心 that has nothing to do with 'conscious' but everything to do with 'heart'?

♪♭♪

I have thought that there is no philosopher of pessimism in China until I came across this remark on Śākyamuni, said to be '要人厌恶人世, 把人生之苦说得无以复加'.¹²³

Which means that he 'wants people to hate life by describing the bitterness of life beyond expression'.

But he was born in Nepal.

Ovid on wives:

> … Leave nagging to wives and husbands,
>   Let them, if they want, think it a natural law,
> A permanent state of feud. Wives thrive on wrangling,
>   That's their dowry… (*The Art of Love*, p. 195)

Why didn't I know about this? Or else.

In 'Tom o' Bedlam's Song', I saw 'my sour face'¹²⁴ and immediately recalled an expression most Chinese patients I interpreted for when describing their backpain as a 'sour pain'.

♪♭♪

A direct quote from Cioran:

> The further one advances into age, the more one runs after honors. Perhaps, in fact, vanity is never more active than on the brink of the grave. One clings to trifles in order not to realize what they

conceal, one deceives nothingness by something even more null and void. (*Drawn and Quartered*, p. 114)

Even the page number is symbolic: 114 (want want death).

♪♩♪

Ordered a book on the recommendation of a writer friend months ago and only just got time to read it. But one of the first sentences about what she thought a hero under Hitler didn't convince me. She said,

Looking back from our vantage point, he is the only person in the entire scene who is on the right side of history.[125]

I put a question mark next to it as a thought came to me: even under Mao, when we all had to show obedience, we were not entirely convinced; we had our doubts; we were defiant at heart; we didn't show it.

Then I thought, he's lucky that he didn't end up getting picked out and put in jail by his Führer.

♪♩♪

Now I saw the 'us' in the subtitle, 'The Lies that Divide Us', I thought, who's 'us'? Have we ever been that part of 'us'? Who are 'we'? Are 'we' ever united with 'us'?

There are always lies, like nights. They may divide some while uniting others. Who can say for certain his or hers won't turn out to be lies down the track? Who has the monopoly on truth?

♪♩♪

I'm beginning to get bored. But this:

Now the skin was haggard on her cheek, the ash of many dead emotions that he hadn't seen. (*The Living and the Dead*, p. 291)

'How did he write like that?' was my question.

♪♩♪

If you are married and have affairs, you openly write about it. Did you do that? Did you publish that? Do you dare? Did you dare?

Joseph Roth did. In a letter to Mr Reifenberg, he said and I quote,

For half a day I worked as a salesman, got drunk at night, and slept with an ugly hotel chambermaid from sheer wretchedness. (*A Life in Letters*, p. 103)

And a few paragraphs after, he talks about his wife that 'is very ill'. (p. 104)

♪♪♪

A comment on Australian women from the early 1970s, with a tinge of Taoism:

All you bloody Aussie women are the same. You're scared to death of making fools of yourselves. (*Don't Talk To Me About Love*, p. 85)

Followed by Paula's thought that she

had always measured acts by their consequences and not their intrinsic being, and had thought everything useless which was not successful, and therefore…had been frozen in a rigid state of do-nothingness. (p. 85)

The Taoism of 'do-nothingness' now gone, replaced with do-everythingness in the Parliament. Nothing at the top sacred any more, maybe never even in the first place.

♪♪♪

Talking about poetry, someone (I forgot who) says in *The Dwarfs* that 'their shit comes out wrapped in silk and satin'. (p. 97)

Much of contemporary Chinese poetry is like that. A lot of Australian poetry, too.

♪♪♪

In *Australian Nicknames*, wife is referred to as 'The Leader of the Opposition'. (p. 68) That recalls a poem I wrote and published more than twenty years ago:

Domestic Politics

my wife is my opposition leader

if i sit on the left
she'll sit on the right

if i lie down on my back
she'll lie down on her belly

if she cooks
i have to do the dishes

if she cleans
i have to tip the rubbish

when she speaks
i keep my mouth shut

when i speak
she keeps hers

as there's no mr speaker
we sometimes speak together

we hold domestic elections
once a month

when she has her period
i exit

then i come back
with a vengeance

verging on violence
while she plays the wilderness again

no one beats the other
we are equal

together we rule this tiny kingdom of ours
like a democracy[126]

That's twenty-four years ago; I did not know about the nickname.

I have always encouraged my son to seek a white woman as his partner, thinking they may be purer materialistically. My Italian friend Frank discouraged my innocent idealism by saying, 'Oh, no, that may not be right. They love money, too.'

As if to prove him right, my daily reading brought my attention to this that goes,

> She wanted to marry a gentleman of leisure; she wanted a European establishment. She wanted her husband to have an English accent, an income of fifty thousand dollars a year from real estate and no ambitions to increase that income. And – she faintly hinted – she did not want much physical passion in the affair. (*The Good Soldier*, p. 60)

Why did I find that so boring?

I was meaning to lead my next book of bilingual Chinese and English poems with this quote that goes,

> It is not the instinct of self-preservation that keeps us going, it is only the impossibility of our seeing the future. Of seeing it? of merely imagining it. If we knew all that lies ahead of us, no one would stoop to persist. Since every future disaster remains abstract, we cannot absorb it. Moreover, we do not even absorb it when it falls upon us and replaces us. (*Drawn and Quartered*, p. 124)

I decided against it because I already have quoted Cioran in that took, titled 《我生活在 3020 年》.

I meant book, not took. But I like the shape of took.

♪♪

I think I'm beginning to understand why intellectuals and writers, Christina Stead one of them, left Australia in droves in those days. I would have gone myself. If there's a better alternative than China and Australia, I would have left the country a long time ago.

The only option for me is fiction. And unpublished, unpublishable. In a country with little future for someone like me.

♪♪

'My friend, Graham, is suffering from depression. His two shops were closed. He owns a property worth six million dollars in Toorak but he's paying mortgage,' said Sunny, my friend.

'Doesn't sound too bad, because he isn't trying to take his own life,' said I.

'But he burst into tears the other day when we met,' said Sunny.

'That's nothing. A friend of mine killed himself in his early forties, apparently for no reason at all. In retrospect, I can see, he never posted anything on WeChat MOMENTS and he never clicks "Like" for anyone's postings. Those were signs.'

'No, they are not. I never post anything and I never click "Like" for anyone. But I never kill myself,' said Sunny.

♪♪

I prefer thinking alone against what Henry Lawson says:

> I like a thinking mate, and I believe that thinking in company is a lot more healthy and more comfortable, as well as less risky, than thinking alone. (*Send Round the Hat*, p. 53)

In all the years I have spent in Australia, the possibility of 'thinking in company' was pretty much nil.

Now it has sunken below zero.

I only talk to books. And think alone.

'Nothing equals a fighter who renounces, nothing rivals the ecstasy of capitulation…' (*Drawn and Quartered*, p. 127)

Immediately I read this, I thought of a poem about the poet knocked down on the floor, lying there without a fight and enjoying the pleasure of lying flat on his back, by Shen Haobo.

That's years ago and now I can't find it.

Eyes and eyelashes. Ban Gu commented on him that Sima Qian was smart enough to know everything but not smart enough to avoid punishment by castration the same way one has eyes to see everything except one's own eyelashes. He uses two words in that comment: 目睫 (eye/lashes).[127]

The difference between the eye and the lashes.

I have come across many women in my life who seemed endowed with a transcendental insight into things that I, as a man, am not able to discern. This is why I quite agree with what I read here:

> The insight of women upon matters of this sort was deeper and more unerring than that of men. It was a woman and not a man who had been filled most completely with the whole fullness of the Deity. (*The Way of All Flesh*, p. 87)

For this reason, and for this reason alone, I'll turn the protagonist of my next novel into a woman.

I don't know who he is but I listened to him playing jazz with his clarinet on YouTube while having a haircut by my wife in my dining room. Afterwards, when I finished and went to the loo, still listening to him while opening *The Dwarfs* to a place where I last stopped, I found this that goes,

The art of dealing with others is one, to be able to see through them, and two, to keep your trap shut. (p. 99)

And a few sentences down, this:

I've discovered an art, Mark said, to find the mind's construction in the arse. (p. 99)

Now, I found that quite jazzy. In fact, I now think, the whole book is like jazz that goes on and on. The person playing clarinet is Tommy Dorsey. I'll check him out shortly.

Came across this: 'I was so one-minded in my purpose', (*The Good Soldier*, p. 63); and thought, how Chinese this is!

Again, it's not as balanced as the Chinese language, in which they say, *yixin yiyi* (one-hearted, one-minded).

In what Lenin said to Gorky, I heard him warn him against 'whimpering over rotten intellectuals'.[128]

I was reminded of what Mao said: 路线错了，知识越多越反动。

Literally, if you take the wrong line, the more knowledge you have, the more reactionary you are.

For many years, I have wanted to put together a collection of poetry to be titled *The Garden of Error*,[129] because I was fascinated by what creative sparks errors and mistakes can lead to.

I had an alternative title for it, too: *Poems of an Errorist*.

Now, I'd like to quote Cioran in part, who says, 'We are all of us in error, the humorists excepted.' (*Drawn and Quartered*, p. 136)

Su Shi talks about Chen Shugu's admiration for himself as a scholar of Buddhism when his servant's remark rings more true when he says that Chen constantly talks about eating dragon's flesh which, according to the servant, is not as good as the pork that he himself eats daily and feels happy about.¹³⁰

And that links in some way to ancient Chinese wisdom that it's far better to give a piece of rope to the drowning person instead of offering a piece of gold to him or it's far better to feed someone starving for a hundred days with something simple than offer him a feast of food. Actually, it's my misreading because it actually goes that it won't do to promise someone a feast of food, not if he has gone starving for a hundred days.

It goes from there that if you run the government and deal with ordinary daily matters you don't need to tackle them theoretically. But you have to deal with them head-on, realistically and matter-of-factly.¹³¹

Now, that seems quite relevant to present-day Australia, a country that seems constantly engaging in a war of words with China, making its own people suffer as a result of Chinese sanctions.

As if to criticise me by implication, a line by Kenneth Koch appears:

> 'No one was supposed to comment on the failings of Soviet industry.' (*The Collected Poems of Kenneth Koch*, p. 522)

I was talking to a poet friend of mine about the daily ordinariness of my poetry and of how I dwell on it in all its variety when, the next day, I came across this in Martin Heidegger that Dasein 'is proximally and for the most part – in its average everydayness'. (*Being and Time*, pp. 37–8)

Now, that seems to suggest to me that poetry itself is Dasein.

'Everything is wrong when done in the name of right.' That's a thought that just flashed through my mind after I read this remark, while standing pissing into the toilet,

Words are finite organs of the infinite mind. They cannot cover the dimensions of what is in truth. They break, chop and impoverish it. An action is the perfection and publication of thought. A right action seems to fill the eye, and to be related to all nature. (Emerson, p. 38)

My liking for him stopped at the words like 'perfection' and 'right'. I can't read him when he sounds righteous. America has since done so much right that is wrong.

Significantly, when I read 'Good Riddance!' (*Drawn and Quartered*, p. 136) I thought I saw 'God Riddance'.
That's what wonders mistakes are capable of working.

He comments on inheritance for life thus:

To leave him [the son] a small independence was perhaps the greatest injury which one could inflict upon a young man. It would cripple his energies, and deaden his desire for active employment. Many a youth was led into evil courses by the knowledge that on arriving at majority he would come into a few thousands. (*The Way of All Flesh*, p. 88)

I know of a poet, one for life, kept alive by his dead banker father with an inexhaustible source of savings, capped at a certain amount per month, a poet about whose poetry I really have little to say.

In his exile, Su Shi, with his wife and kids, suffered greatly, to such a degree that his wife got so angry with the awful treatment meted out to them by the local authorities that she, while saying all the disasters were a result of his passion for books, burnt many of his manuscripts, with the result that 70 to 80% of his manuscripts or books was gone.[132]

I had a curious feeling when I read that. My feeling was that my wife, Australia, did something similar to that in that she declined my offer of manuscripts for sale or donation through its excruciatingly nasty library system.

♪♪

The character in Thomas Hardy's story 'For Conscience' Sake' is dissatisfied with himself being 'a specimen of the heap of flesh called humanity'. (*Life's Little Ironies*, p. 38)

Know what that reminded me of? The Chinese translation of *David Copperfield* by Lin Shu, who, without a word of English, managed to translate the whole book with the interpreting assistance of his friend Wei Yi, as something titled *kuairou yusheng ji* or 《块肉余生记》, or, literally, *An Account of How the Heap of Flesh Was Left Alive*.

♪♪

It's not till forty years after I first began writing that I realise, perhaps for a thousandth time, that, for someone like me, writing can't be otherwise than failure, a word with a 'lure' in it.

Yesterday, when I went to the city to meet Michael, a former student, now a friend, I put two books in my bag, *Drawn and Quartered* and *Life's Little Ironies*. I read the first one and found something to my liking, and hereby I quote it:

> 'Your book is a failure.' – 'No doubt, but you are forgetting that I wanted it to be one, and that it could hardly be a success otherwise.' (p. 141)

♪♪

Michael is one of the few former students who took to reading after he graduated from the school where I taught him. When I checked with him whether he was still reading and what kind of books he read, he said history, politics, non-fiction in the main, and cartoons as well.

'You need to add philosophy to that list,' said I. Then I showed the book to him for him to take a mobile phone photograph to check it out afterwards.

'Pessimistic philosophy the best,' added I.

🎵🎵

When Cioran said, 'Life is more and less than boredom, though it is in boredom and by boredom that we discern what life is worth,' (p. 139) I put down in the margins these words: 'Cf. 我早期的无聊诗.' Then these: '可写一本小书: On Boredom.'

🎵🎵

The word 'macabre', when I saw it in 'Macabre obsessions afford no impediment to sexuality' (*Drawn and Quartered*, p. 139), caused me to think I had seen 'Macbeth'. In that instant, I thought to myself, I must write a book, to be titled *On Mistakes*.

🎵🎵

'arson in her heart.' (*The Erotic Poems*, p. 201)

Compare that to 《心藏大恶》 (*xin cang da e*), or *Great Evil Hidden in the Heart*, by Shen Haobo, and write a comment of however many words if you like, and if you were my student.

🎵🎵

It's a bit too late now, as the novel was already self-published. But if I do another edition, I might include this as one of the leading quotes, ahead of the main text of the book:

> We should have to suppose that the desire to murder is actually present in the unconscious and that neither taboos nor moral prohibitions are psychologically superfluous but that on the contrary they are explained and justified by the existence of an ambivalent attitude towards the impulse to murder. (*Totem and Taboo*, p. 70)

I meant my novel *West of the River*, one single copy published in 2020.

🎵🎵

Everything points to the present, even something published as early as 1915, in a book where it goes, with the Old Hurlbird talking of Paris as 'full of snakes in the grass', and 'with the aspiration that all American women should one day be sexless…' (*The Good Soldier*, p. 65) Isn't that what one should aspire to in Australia after what happened in the Parliament?

♪♪♪

When I read the following, you know what I was reminded of and also ask what it puts you in mind of?

> When I happen to be satisfied with everything, even with God and myself, I immediately react like the man who, on a brilliant day, torments himself because the sun is bound to explode in a few billion years. (*Drawn and Quartered*, p. 142)

I was reminded of Li Bai, who has two lines that go, from memory: 人生不满百，常怀千岁忧。
One lives a life less than a hundred years but one worries a worry as long as a millennium.

♪♪♪

As far as I understand it, 'How to endure oneself,' as asked by Cioran, is the core of boredom.

The Japanese young, angry with themselves and with the world at large, seem to have a solution: staying behind a closed door for decades.

♪♪♪

I read Terry Eagleton's *On Evil* years ago. And I don't remember anything of it. It takes a single remark from Cioran to beat the whole book when he says,

> What is evil? It is what is done with a view to happiness in this world. (*Drawn and Quartered*, p. 144)

♪♪♪

The story would have to be too long if told in the traditional way. Simplified, it tells of a poet having a field day when he hears the downfall of his party boss and told me so.

My immediate response to that is, if you weren't a poet, you would probably have collided with him and got yourself in the deep shit.

Admittedly, there is something incorruptible about poets even though they have little ability to attract any gold dust, and corrupt cases involving poets seem relatively few.

I'm talking about China, a nation of huge corruption.

♪♭♪

Someone claimed that English originated in Chinese. I read the book but I forgot the title and the author. But it's easy to find that claim, right now and right here: https://zhuanlan.zhihu.com/p/82466030

This was prompted by the phrase I found today in that nicknames dictionary: 'hundreds and thousands'. (Such a matching expression for the Chinese: 成百上千! (hundreds thousands)

♪♭♪

In reading 《红楼梦》, either because of my weakening eyesight or because the character '家' is not clearly printed, I saw this – '宝钗来至冢中'[133] and thought it says, 'Baochai came to the grave.'

Why? Because the character '冢' (grave), looks very much like the character '家' (home). I recorded it because this is the first time I took note of it in my sixty-five years of life and also because I found the two to have quite an eerie affinity.

♪♭♪

I found something that I could use as the title of my next novel or poetry collection: 'that accursed country'. (*A Life in Letters*, p. 108)

If published, it should look like this, in bold:

That Accursed Country

♪♭♪

In 《西游记》,[134] there are two lines that go, 只须下苦功，扭出铁中血。(My translation: If you work hard enough, you can wring blood out of iron.)

Yes, but not out of Australia.

♪♪

Don't like recording dreams any more, let alone write them into poetry, like I used to before. Had two dreams last night, one earlier than the latter. In the early one, the male poet, in a reading he gives, taunts a woman poet outside the door, both in a loud voice and both I personally know. In the latter dream, she and I have just finished our business, in a city whose name is lost to us, and I am about to mobile-phone-check for details about the Hubei Long Distance Coach Station to head back to Hubei when I realise there's no such thing, as we are probably in Shanghai. Then the idea suggests itself to me that we should try to hail a taxi or, alternatively, Didi, Uber's China version.

The city, in that instant, becomes very bare and grey.

Mini-report. The writer now is living his dream. He posts stuff, poetry mainly, on his blog, on a daily basis. From where he can see, at the back, the number of people who read it is zero, for days on end. And he remains unperturbed.

Just saw this poem, by someone I know:

8.47 a.m.

> Don't ever talk, to me, about, australia, such a rotten coun,try
> You had great. hope. when you first came
> Your hope was dashed. Again. And. Again
> You wondered. if. you, had come, to a hell
> You wondered, if, it is more, worth.while leaving than living
> You looked. around. and saw white bones making. money
> You saw. bones of colour, too
> You had all there was to it a sky, that, keeps, saying, to, you You people. You are never good. Enough. For. Us
> You talk back saying: you hell! You Hell! YOU HELL!
> You put me to death for life: You Hell

♪♪

When I read 'The winter nights that are so cold', in Thomas Wyatt's 'My lute awake!',[135] I thought of my own poem, 'moon over melbourne', with its line 'with a man-made light that is not only cold'.[136]

The book is dedicated to Ouyang Binyu, as I just found out.

When she said that 'The election would set the United States on a course toward isolationism, tribalism, the walling in and protecting of one's own, the worship of wealth and acquisition at the expense of others',[137] (emphasis my own) I wrote my comment next to it in the margins:

不一直都是这样吗?又不是 21 世纪的新事!

♪♪

In Hardy's story 'A Tragedy of Two Ambitions', when the two sons lose their mother's hard-won money through their father's dissipation, Joshua the older brother says, 'But we can't rise!'[138]

That sounds oddly familiar to me, in two senses. When I was their age, 'rise' as a word was never part of my ambition; I didn't even have an ambition, I don't think. Coming from my background, I would have regarded 'rise' as vulgarly materialistic. Indeed, when I graduated from the university and found a steady job in a big organisation as a translator and interpreter, I was hopeless because I could see no change at the end of the road twenty or thirty years after. I just wanted to quit the job in pursuit of my own interests. And I did, only two years into it.

Su Shi describes Su Zhe, his younger brother, as someone who 心不异口, 口不异心, 心即是口, 口即是心.

In my translation, that is,

> Su Zhe has a heart that is the same as his mouth, a mouth that is the same as his heart, a heart that is the mouth and a mouth that is the heart.

Slightly altered, this becomes more English when it incorporates the mind:

> Su Zhe has a mind that is the same as his mouth, a mouth that is the same as his mind, a mind that is the mouth and a mouth that is the mind.

A bit scary because he must be someone who speaks his mind. Or heart, Chinese-wise. Do you dare do that in China? Do you even dare do that in Australia? The problem with me after living in Australia for over thirty years is that I have become more and more reluctant to speak my mind because, if you want to know, everyone is so correct around me.

By the way, Su Shi, Su Zhe and Su Xun, Su Shi's father, three well-known men of letters in the Northern Song dynasty, were known as the Three Sus.

♪♪

Only a few days ago, I saw this that goes,

> Everything is nothing, including the consciousness of nothing. (*Drawn and Quartered*, p. 144)

And, today, as if to prove the point, my external hard drive went dead, with all my writings, fiction, non-fiction, poetry and criticism, in both English and Chinese, that could fill scores of books.

Now, nothing is everything. The taunting voice seems to say, if you are overproductive, you overkill yourself.

♪♪

I now am in no mood to turn these lines I like into poetry, such as 'A man without a present tense' (ibid., p. 146), and 'the secretary of my sensations'. (Ibid., p. 148)

♪♪

Again, in 'A Tragedy of Two Ambitions', by Thomas Hardy, I find something so Chinese when Joshua advises his brother to 'make a good impression upon' the sub-dean because 'that was everything' (p. 56), because he seems echoing what my mother always advised me to do when young, never leaving a bad impression upon people.

As I grow nearer my death, I realise more and more that people are the same by nature regardless of their skin colour, language and culture.

♪♪♪

Su Shi, in a letter to his friend, wonders in these words:

人命脆促，真在呼吸间耶?[139]

In my translation:

Life is so fragile and short that it really comes and goes between breathings?

♪♪♪

Just now, a thought suggested itself to me that I am a professional obituary-writer who has just composed an obituary for a close friend in the projected lead-up to his death.

♪♪♪

The death of my external hard drive led to a spoken-poem on my mobile phone this morning,

《突然》

譬如一根碗口粗的绳子，突然在某天断掉

譬如某个健壮的汉子，突然被风击中，嘴歪了

譬如海水在天上飘着，突然一条比牙齿还小的鱼掉下来了

譬如50年前写的一个字，突然从地下冒出，对你说：就是我

譬如早就被删除的图片和录像，突然以某种奇异的方式，再度在眼角浮现

譬如从头上飞过的鸟，双翅突然断掉

譬如还未出生的人，突然还未出生

譬如天上的声音，突然被人间听见了

譬如在水面上写字，突然有人踩水过来了

譬如有封信突然来到，里面传来未曾听说过的信息

譬的如，突的然

譬了如，突了然

譬是如，突不是然

    I admit I can't possibly translate the last three stanzas or lines because I run out of abilities. It's like my other poem 《尔兰的雨》.

    Now that my hard drive is dead, I can't find it any more.

Read this:

> Statements…are bound, therefore, to annoy certain readers and to push Brodsky still further to the margins of the regnant discourse… Yet we should also recall that he has never sought solidarity with any group or 'interpretive community' other than his own private 'dead poets' society…[140]

    Know why I include this? Reason being I thought he was talking about me, particularly when 'solidarity' is mentioned.

    This is a book that I'm actually translating at the moment, contract already signed.

Risk. I hear you. And I have run it, to the degree of.

    Now, hear what David M. Bethea has to say on Broad Sky, no, I mean Brodsky:

> The Christian sacrifice that stands at the center of Broadsky's poetic worldview and the tradition he inherited does not consist merely of toil – the 'Forward, my loyal ox' of Valery Bryusov's famous credo – but of *risk*, of giving of oneself without the guarantee of recompense.[141]

Ah, well. But the 'Christian sacrifice' – it sounds so irrelevant, to me at least.

I bought a book yesterday for thirty-three bucks. Not on Kevin's advice, but just because he happened to mention it when I talked about Australia's long history of fear towards China, resulting in book after book of Chinese invasion.

My very first experience with the book is not a pleasant one. The first two pages of praises for the author's previous award-winning book is a total turn-off and unnecessary. The third page, another one of praises, contains a word that is deliberately vague, and pathetic: 'translated into numerous languages'. One simply wants to know, how many?

A remark, made on WeChat Moments, yesterday in Chinese, by a writer friend in Shanghai, comes back. It says,

有很多文学奖，对作家来说，不是奖掖而是毒害。不得也罢!

In my translation, it goes,

There are many literary awards that are more poisonous than rewarding to writers; one'd rather go without them.

I told her this that I've just read:

There are some things that it is good to forget. Indeed, I have lived long enough to learn that it is a great part of wisdom to know what to forget.[142]

Selective forgetfulness is good if we can achieve it. But sometimes certain things refuse to go away, like love made.

'笔冻。写不成字。'[143] Su Shi said in a letter to his friend.

'My inkbrush is frozen and I can't write a word.' Su Shi says in that letter and in my translation.

It's like what I said to a friend recently in a WeChat message, 'I can't find the document as my external hard drive has crashed and it is getting fixed at the moment.'

Many centuries apart, and yet, we still are stuck with the basic when it comes to the tools of writing.

♪♪

When I saw this, I said, 'I'll keep it and write a poem with it as a title or about it.' This:

'It was a cloud no bigger than a man's hand.' (*Life's Little Ironies*, p. 64)

The next day when I picked the book up again, the urge was lost; I no longer wanted to write anything.

♪♪

I described the poem to her, 'To Urania', particularly the last two lines,

Yet until brown clay has been crammed down my larynx, / only gratitude will be gushing from it.[144]

Her immediate reaction is, 'That's a lie. It's almost like saying, "If you kill all my family members, parents, brothers and sisters, I won't ever hate you. In fact, I'll love you all the more."'

♪♪

When Sun Wukong, the Monkey King, arrives with Pigsy and Longevity Monk at a river they can't cross, the eight-hundred-li flowing sand river, the water is referred to as 弱水, weak water, even though it is so strong and expansive that no one can cross it without the aid of Buddha.

In a way, it is as difficult to translate it into English as you do when you translate 'dry water', an expression used in 'To Urania' by Brodsky, into Chinese because there are no such Chinese equivalents unless you render a direct translation.

♪♪

On the other hand, regarding the word 'gratitude' in the Brodsky poem, referred to before, I do empathise with him because all the suffering he sustained in the Soviet Union is a wealth of wealth to him as a poet.

In the West, where no such suffering is possible, people commit suicide in a well-off state.

You may notice I wrote 'a wealth of wealth'. That's only because I am the I who writes the way only the I can do.

The latest report: I have finished reading this book and have marked my impressions in three places in my language, as follows:

完全没有任何感觉，很快翻完。(2021.5.17 夜洗脚时) (p. 187)
一分钟不到翻完。(p. 310)
一分钟不到翻完。2021.5.17 夜翻完于洗脚时 (p. 434)

I have taken a photograph of these markings.¹⁴⁵

According to Solzhenitsyn, Russian poet Tanya Khodkevich got 'a ten-year sentence for these verses':

You can pray *freely*
But just so God alone can hear.¹⁴⁶

Slightly better than I, sentenced to a thirty-year sentence in this country where a PhD thesis is an illusory degree that condemns one to stay outside the universities for life.

Not saying thank you would leave him unfulfilled and upset for hours, sometimes even days, when he went to teach in a Chinese university in Shanghai. Soon enough he found, most people hardly ever say thank you, not even his students, BA or MA, who would simply reply to his emails or WeChat instructions or help with a 'got it'.

Now, he was once again reminded of that when he read this, in Joseph Roth's *The Emperor's Tomb*, where 'I' wanted to thank him, but how pitiful thanks would have sounded, thanks from my mouth! It occurred to me how often in my life I had mechanically uttered the word thanks. I had dishallowed it. (p. 106)

♪♪

Perhaps it's the way he writes like me or I write like him that prompted me to translate him as early as the early 1980s when I was still a university student in my mid to late twenties.

Now, in my mid-sixties, I found something he wrote similar to something I wrote. He writes, 'She said I'll kill anyone who writes me a poem.'[147]

I write, in 'The poet's wife', 'once told the poet: / never write about me / or else i'll kill you.'[148]

I don't know when he wrote his. But I do know I wrote mine in the early 1990s in Melbourne; I didn't read his at the time of my writing, mine subsequently published in Swedish translation. Big deal.

♪♪

Translating this book,[149] I saw this: 'Writers' homes become landmarks by which average citizens take their bearing' in Russia and thought of how someone pointed out a property by the roadside saying Xavier Herbert had lived there years ago in Townsville, the property already sold many times over, and how someone wrote to me about the status of writers in Hong Kong as no less than dogs. Or did he say that there were more men of letters or characters than dogs in Hong Kong?

And the overriding thought, right now: no one in Australia will give a fuck where I live until I won't give a damn if anyone cares, either.

♪♪

This remark, 'all the literary dogs are yapping',[150] instantly recalls that remark above about literary men being dogs in Hong Kong.

♪♪

Much of Australian fiction, contemporary or otherwise, is unreadable, like Australia's food. Very occasionally, one finds stuff that is interesting, like this below,

> People tearing each other apart. George and Sonia. Maria and her husband. She and Graeme. Did people really use each other, she wondered? Is that what marriage finally became: an unending struggle, a duel, a steady devouring of each other? Was all that Battle of the Sexes theory right after all? It didn't seem fair: that all that hope and expectation, and in their case all that trying, should come down to two people using each other.[151]

Part of the reason, I think, is that in Australia few dare speak their mind, all wanting to maintain a sham veneer of perfection and nothing that goes awry.

When I read this:

> The ownmost meaning of Being which belongs to the inquiry into Being as an historical inquiry, gives us the assignment [Anweisung] of inquiring into the history of that inquiry itself, that is, of becoming historiological.' (*Being and Time*, p. 42)

My comment, written in the margins next to it, goes, 绝对 ZNJJ 的哲学。

In *The Emperor's Tomb*, 'T's mother's piano is empty, all its strings removed. According to her, "I wanted to force myself to stop playing."' (p. 110)

It was this remark that caused me to remember something similar. During the pandemic year of 2020, I experienced an overproduction of poetry. Every time I went out on my daily walk, poetry came to me, right, left and centre, and kept me busy all day long.

To stop myself from poetry, I had to find a way and I soon found it: my earpiece cord, with which I listened to massive music from YouTube, drowning myself in it, jazz, pop songs, clarinet, bassoon, indeed, all sorts, managing in the end to cut down the size of poetry, but not as successfully as the mother who had her piano disembowelled.

♪♪♪

Paid a visit to a local artist whose paintings of amalgamations, or plagiarisms, or remixings, in my words, I'm going to write about, and heard him talk about the Monkey as a part source of his painterly inspiration.

Now, I am reading the novel in Chinese, reaching page of 272 of a 1,160-pager. A few lines caught my eye that go,

色乃伤身之剑，贪之必定遭殃。佳人二八好容妆，更比夜叉凶壮。

A rough approximation of mine goes,

Sex is a sword that harms health
And indulgence in it leads to ruins
A girl who looks great when made up
Is more ferocious than a hideous hag

♪♪♪

Confucius says,

君子以行言，小人以舌言。

I say, in translation,

A gentleman speaks with action whereas a little man speaks with his tongue.

Or:

A gentleman's words are his action and a small man's words are his tongue.

♪♪♪

When I read this line, 'Each care decays, and yet my sorrow springs,'[152] this came to mind: 伤春诗.

A subgenre in Chinese poetry that depicts how sad and sorrowful the coming of spring makes one feel, it nevertheless literally means, or is capable of meaning, wounding-spring poetry, hurt spring poetry, poetry of wounded spring, poetry of hurting spring, poetry of saddened and saddening spring, et cetera.

♪♪♪

Years ago, I learnt that when they translated the Chinese classic *The Golden Lotus*, the French translators would put the sexually offensive bits in Latin. In a way, translation in a foreign language would render the real stuff less real and, perversely, more learned.

There is a more recent instance of that when John Roth comments on André Gide, in a letter to Reifenberg. Towards the end, he wrote,

> Was asked later what I thought of Gide. *C'est un acteur, n'est-ce pas?* – said Paulhan. And I: *Il est plus qu'un acteur, il est une actrice.* (*A Life in Letters*, p. 115)

I had a good laugh. Here, I have a lot to thank my limited command of French for.

♪♪♪

Let me stop here to do damage to writing as I am, right at this moment, sick of it, with a direct quote or two, from Cioran:

> Old age, after all, is merely the punishment for having lived. (*Drawn and Quartered*, p. 167)

And

> Hope is the normal form of delirium. (Ibid., p. 167)

Feeling better now, both applied, and applying.

♪♪♪

妙玉 has a good way of putting it when she talks about how to eat tea in 《红楼梦》.

If you drink one cup, that is taste. If you drink two, that's the stupidity of merely allaying the thirst. If you drink three, it's just feeding the donkey. (p. 266 in the Chinese version)

Her solution to good-quality water is extreme: a jug of water melted from the snow on the winter plums five years ago in a temple, preserved under ground since.

Only page 16 reached, this book that I bought for thirty-three dollars, has to be the boringest I have ever come across even though it's surrounded with praises.

In fact, the more praises, the more boring. That can almost be a current yardstick for any published books.

天意: the mind of the sky.

I went to the post office. Peter said, 'There's nothing.' We talked a bit about the resurgence of new cases even in late May 2021, when the quick dialogue slid to Andrews, who was still recovering from his fall. That's when Peter said, half-jokingly, 'Blame Jenny.' Both of us burst out laughing, I, in particular, realising the balance set: one fall followed by another, in this case, a fall from her position that led to a physical fall, neither related to the other.

When she heard this, my wife said, 'That's tianyi, 天意,' which is the sky of the mind, oh, no, I mean the mind of the sky.

I like Joseph Roth when he is dismissive about his contemporaries, such as Ulitz, saying in a letter to Bertaux, that their 'Morals: excellent. Mental capacity: below average. Industry: praiseworthy.'[153]

In that novel, when the cossacks go to find a stream to drink, the water is described 'as fresh as children's tears'.[154]

In *Journey to the West*, there is a ginseng fruit that flowers in 3,000 years, bears fruit in another 3,000 years and ripens in still another 3,000 years and one has to wait till 10,000 years to eat it. But there are only thirty pieces of fruit in the shape of little babies. If you take the smell of one piece of fruit, you'll live to 360 years of age and if you eat one, you will live for 47,000 years.[155]

That's pure fiction. One knows and one keeps reading. It is for this reason that I forgave the boast about a bridge of 'a curved six-lane single span' built between Hobart and 'a remote island with a population of only six hundred'.[156]

A quote, from a story I'm reading, about a character by the name of Mr Jolliffe:

A son of the town, his parents had died when he was quite young…[157]

I think it needs pruning. No?

Emerson's words that 'Children, it is true, believe in the external world'[158] caused me to pause in my tracks as I thought I had seen them 'believe in the external hard drive.'

This book, priced at US$7.99, cost me thirty Chinese yuan, far less than what they charged me for recovering data in a recently crashed external hard drive of mine.

I have been lately engaging in another self-initiated project that I tentatively call 'Tree dating Project'. It's a simple enough idea that one can put into practice as long as one can execute it on a daily basis: writing down the date, including the day of the week and the date of the day, month and year, on the tree bark one happens to go past on his daily walk-rounds. What I wrote with a red marker today was 'Lockdown Day 2: Saturday 29/05/2021'.

Then this from Cioran:

> Every project is a camouflaged form of slavery. (*Drawn and Quartered*, p. 175)

I had to laugh at my own slavish self.

If there is anything good about Australia, it is its obsession with PC. First, they do it wrong. Then they correct it and feel good about it. Then, years after, they realise they've done wrong again when they felt they did it correctly. Hence the circle that recycles itself, viciously, obnoxiously.

A philosophical directive against it might have to come from Cioran who says, among other things,

> Nothing corrects us for anything. (*Drawn and Quartered*, p. 175)

Most of the time, it is the simplest things that catch attention, like this:

> 'You know,' he said, 'babies come so suddenly; one goes to bed one night and next morning there is a baby.'[159]

While Heidegger's obsession with being is such a waste of time for me, I have persisted till page 47, fourteen years after I first bought it, on 16 June 2007, when I found something that makes sense where he says,

> But createdness…was an essential item in the structure of the ancient conception of Being. (*Time and Being*, p. 46)

That, to me, is no more than 生, containing both 'birthing' and 'born', as part of being. Or 病, a condition that is born in the birthing and that persists till the end, uncurable except by death.

But Cioran wouldn't have anything to do with it as he says,

> I have never been able to find out what being means, except some-

times in eminently nonphilosophical moments. (*Drawn and Quartered*, p. 171)

Both Cioran and I talked about people dying young, at different times, unaware of each other. He said,

> He who has not had the good luck to die young will leave only a caricature of his pride behind. (*Drawn and Quartered*, p. 173)

I said something to Kris some time ago to this effect that when you die young, say, at forty, none of your photos left behind will be old, as compared with those of you when you die old, say, at eighty. Granted you have lots left, but many of them will show age. At the time I said that, I hadn't read the Cioran remark above.

When I came across George Herbert's poem on Man, one stanza, the second, is more than enough:

> Nothing hath got so far
> But man has caught and kept it as his prey;
> His eyes dismont the hightest star:
> He is in little all the sphere.
> Herbs gladly cure our flesh, because that they
> Find their acquaintance there.[160]

Yes, everything is to serve his purpose until everything dies or languishes. How far has Man corrupted the earth around him? What water in nature is not heavily polluted? I'm sick of this Man, and of myself. But I can't do anything.

According to Robert Menzies, Winston Churchill, when in power, was a 'bad listener' and 'was reputed to dislike opposition'.[161]

I'm glad he brought this to my attention because, in my opinion, no man in power is not like that, least of all emperors and kings, in ancient or recent China, to which no Western male counterparts are an exception.

♪♪♪

Years ago, at university, I read *The Vicar of Wakefield* by Oliver Goldsmith. Then, in my early days in Australia, I wrote the poem 'Going mad', with a line that goes, 'or I imagine vicariously the state of a convict hundreds of years ago'.[162]

It was not till yesterday when, reading Samuel Butler, I realised that the two words are interrelated, as shown in this instance about the life of a clergyman:

> This is why the clergyman is so often called a vicar – he being the person whose vicarious goodness is to stand for that of those entrusted to his charge.[163]

♪♪♪

Listen to this woman say to a man about women,

> You've got a career, ambition, success to sustain you. And you can still be attractive to women at sixty, at the age when most women have to buy their sex.[164]

If you ask me if it's true, I ask who? But I find it interesting.

♪♪♪

Confucius says,

> 君子博学深谋而不遇时者，众矣，何独丘哉。且芝兰生于深林，不以无人而不芳。

And I translate:

When a gentleman has great learning and deep vision but is not found employable, he's not the only one as there are many like him, me no exception. After all, when irises and orchids grow in the depths of a forest, they don't stop being fragrant because they are not noticed.

I love this.

♪♪

Isabella Whitney's poem 'A Communication Which the Author Had to London Before She Made Her Will' has a few lines that go,

> No, no, thou never did'st me good,
>   nor ever will, I know.
> Yet am I in no angry mood,
>   but will, or ere I go.[165]

I thought they have faint echoes to someone in his relationship to Australia, someone like me.

♪♪

You'd think there is a radical difference between the English and the Chinese. And you'd be wrong thus thinking. According to Samuel Butler,

> There are two classes of people in this world, those who sin, and those who are sinned against; if a man must belong to either, he had better belong to the first than to the second.[166]

Even as I recall Shakespeare's 'more sinned against than sinning', I remember a more apt remark by Cao Cao, the great man of letters and military strategist, in the Eastern Han Dynasty:

宁可我 负天下人，不可天下人负我。

Meaning? If more Englishly put,

I'd rather be sinning than sinned against.

Put Chinesely,

I'd rather sin against all under heaven than being sinned against by them.

♪♪

The word 'Chinese', as a signpost, is often used by Australian writers. The way Heather Rose talks about 'three Chinese women' (*Bruny*, p. 57) without going to any physical detail reminds me of Chinese people written about by Jessica Anderson in her *The Impersonators* (1980) and bothers me although it could be a suggestion that next time I write a novel about Australia I could drop the word 'Australian' here and there indiscriminately, too?

♪♪♪

Squatter, a nickname for someone, usually a female, who 'sits around the office all day reading magazines'[167] ignited a memory, long forgotten, of a mouth slider (顺口溜) about the old days in China, in the 1970s and 1980s:

一杯茶，一包烟，一张报纸看一天。

Literally:

a cup of tea, a pack of cigarettes and a newspaper lasts a whole day.

With a difference, though: my day, in a big organisation where I worked as a translator and interpreter, started with bowel movements in the loo, in the company of other early birds.

♪♪♪

An interesting illumination. According to a Nigerian-born playwright, there are 'no black people in Africa', the reason being 'They are not black. They are just themselves.'[168]

That seems to tally with an impression I had when reading Wole Soyinka's poetry and Ben Okri's novel *The Famished Road*, that 'black' as a reference to people's skin colour is not seen anywhere. Blackness is part of their natural being. They don't see it, don't feel it, don't accentuate it. It's only when they go out of their continent that they are recognised as being different, then discriminated against.

Why don't we recognise nights as unacceptably different before we decide to discriminate against them? Is white a colour or non-colour?

♪♪♪

Someone questioned the validity of my remark, made in my reply to a recent interview question, as follows:

Q. What does being Asian-Australian mean to you?
A. It means you don't have a friend in this country.[169]

I didn't bother replying to that person's email. I want to remind her, though, that Wang Ji has written a self-written obituary, 《自撰墓志铭》, or a self-written epitaph, that begins with these words: 有父母，无朋友。(I have parents and I don't have friends.)

Wang Ji, a Chinese poet (585–644), must have written that at least before 644, compared with mid-2020 when I gave an interview that ends with that answer.

I don't know why I get cross every time someone mentions that he or she is 'marking'. By and by, I realise it sounds like a privilege that sets him or her apart from me, they being privileged to mark student papers whereas I do not have such privileges. Soon enough, I got it all sorted out in my heart: this country, ever since I got my PhD in early 1995, has barred me from practising as a lecturer in a university, never ever having the opportunity to 'mark' people, to pay my bills for 'marking' people.

If I used to be nastily called an 'angry Chinese poet', I had a reason; I still have the reason to remain angry. You can't expect people to remain silent and happy while you sentence them to death in life, academic death in my case, can you?

I was relieved to know today, in translating *Joseph Brodsky and the Creation of Exile*, that Dante was an angry man. See this below:

> Dante is a poor man. Dante is an internal *raznochinets* (the 'upstart intellectual' whom Mandelstam had cited as model for himself and his generation in *Noise of Time*) of ancient Roman blood. What is characteristic of him is not at all civility (*liubeznost*), but something quite the opposite. One has to be a blind mole not to notice that during the entire *Divina Commedia* Dante is unable to behave himself, does not know how to proceed, what to say, how to bow.[170]

Then, according to Mandelstam,

the entire charm of the *Commedia* derives precisely from the pathos of this awkwardness and 'internal anxiety,' this inability of the 'tormented and driven man' to fit in and find a place for himself in the 'social hierarchy'. (p. 59)

Exactly! Who can fit in if the society is meant to exclude him for good, as in my case, as in Dante's case?

A German text translated into English that I find could somehow improve.

Example 1: 'When would she have used it last?'[171]
Improvement: 'When was the last time she used it?'

Example 2: 'At that time she liked to follow that…'[172]
Improvement: 'Back then, she liked to follow that…'

Whatever.

According to Robert Menzies, a prime minister by the name of William Morris Hughes, who I have never heard of, 'followed a variety of occupations, teacher, locksmith, umbrella repairer, stage supernumerary, waterside worker…',[173] and that list prompted me to write a list poem, in Chinese, today, as I recalled how many occupations I followed myself: peasant, truck driver, translator, interpreter, language instructor, postdoctoral fellow, professor, and always student.

I have to be honest, at least with myself. I now find Emerson a bore. I do like what he says here when he says, 'Europe has always owed to oriental genius its divine impulse.'[174] But I have lost track of what he means by 'This thought' when he says,

> This thought dwelled always deepest in the minds of men in the devout and contemplative East; not alone in Palestine, where it reached its purest expression, but in Egypt, in Persia, in India, in China. (Same book, p. 112)

I tried a few times but in vain, still not sure what 'This thought' exactly is.

Since I read *A Rebours*, by Joris-Karl Huysmans, in which much smell is smelled, I haven't come across much smell elsewhere. This arvo I did, in *Cindie*, where a description is given:

> Solely coloured labour, she [Blanche] soon realized, would throw upon herself the responsibility for the multifarious tasks connected with provisioning and superintending the Kanakas, whose close approach she could not suffer. Why the body of the Kanaka, especially when sweating, should be offensively odorous, and the Australian Aborigine, apparently much lower in the anthropological scale, smell sweet as a nut, puzzled her. But there it was.[175]

I remember a reference in an Australian story I discussed in my PhD thesis, published in 2008, to Chinese smelling of rice, and a Chinese friend running a shop in which he would always spray the air with a deodorant spray to expel the strong pungent smells left by the white customers.

Solzhenitsyn talks about 'those same spineless, slushy intellectuals' who hardly ever 'vote against' the government.[176]

An apt description of most Chinese intellectuals I have read about or met. Actually, one Russian poet I met in Kazakhstan in 2018 when I was there attending a poetry festival did not answer my question about Putin; instead, he raised his right fist in the air, for a few times, his face remaining wooden and dark. I laughed and gave up trying.

《周礼》or *The Rites of Zhou* is a book that appeared in the second century BC. Among other things, it talks about five types of spies: 因间、内间、反间、生间、死间。[177]

I don't think I'll tell you what they mean. It's more than enough to know that such categories were established already more than 2,000 years ago.

♪♪♪

I agree with Alexis de Tocqueville when he said that the 'surface of American society is covered with a layer of democratic paint'.[178] Same with Australia. Same with all the democracies, there being so many lies around for centuries. We cheat ourselves only when we think we are the best.

♪♪♪

In *Australian Nicknames* I found one, 'Squirrel', that refers to a 'lady who once had bank accounts spread all over the country'.[179]

They probably don't know that this equally applies to corrupt Chinese officials with bank accounts of millions of dollars not only spread across the country but also cross the world, often not in their own names.

♪♪♪

I'm reading 《中国知青事典》, [180] a large book of 926 pages, that begin with a number of photographs showing the educated youths in the 1960s and 1970s.

I can't help noticing 'the number of smiling faces', a remark made by an American engineer in the 1980s when I interpreted for him in YVPO, Yangtze Valley Planning Office, the chief planning office of the Three Gorges Dam. He said, and I recall, thirty-seven years after, that when he was out walking on a Wuhan street, he couldn't help noticing 'the number of smiling faces'.

In the Western discourse, the Cultural Revolution, with all its paraphernalia and consequences, was the ultimate evil. However, those smiling faces were real. I remembered them. I was one of them. I had my hard times. I had my happy times, like everywhere else. Why China? Why pick on China as if it were pure hell?

The number of smiling faces in those photographs. That's what caught my attention when I opened this book.

🎵🎵

Why does one feel sad when it comes to writing, to the writing of books?

I don't know. But my latest discovery, actually more than a decade old, is that the Chinese character 书 (books, pronounced 'shu') sounds exactly like the Chinese character for 输 (defeat, failure, loss, pronounced also 'shu').

You never win when it comes to books. Which is probably why it's called 'boo/k' which sounds very much like the Chinese characters 不可 (bu ke, not possible or can't).

🎵🎵

You only need one sentence to recall something lost in a totally different context. How about this when Samuel Butler says,

> The pair said not a word to one another.[181]

The pair, that is, Mr Theobald and Mrs Theobald, riding in a carriage at dusk, each thinking his or her own thoughts.

What I recalled was a scene in Shennongjia a few years ago where she and I went to visit together on a tour. Most of the time, I realised, we didn't say a single word to each other. I took notice but never told her of my observation.

🎵🎵

Crap, I mean the following:

> But the fellow talked like a cheap novelist. Or like a very good novelist for the matter of that, if it's the business of a novelist to make you see things clearly.[182]

Sorry, mate, I don't want to 'see things clearly' in a novel by a 'good novelist'. I want imagination that takes you to places. I want to hear things. I want to see innovative stuff. Merely 'see(ing) things clearly' is 1915.

♪♪

Ovid says,

> Music unheard gives little joy.[183]

Keats is better in that regard, for he says,

> Heard melodies are sweet, but those unheard are sweeter.

Writing poetry is to do the impossible, to hear unheard music.

♪♪

But Ovid has his good moments, as when he says,

> ... What else do our dedicated poets
>   Pursue but fame? This is the goal of all
> Our labours. Poets were once the chosen of gods and monarchs:
>   In olden times their choirs
> Won great rewards: high honour, a venerable title,
>   These a bard had – plus large
> And regular cash donations. Take Ennius: born a Cababrian
>   Peasant, yet interred in the Scipio family vault
> Because of his art. Today, though, the ivy lies unhonoured,
>   And a life of poetic toil
> Gets you labelled a drone. Still, to slave for recognition
>   Does help. If the *Iliad*, that immortal work,
> Had never been published, who'd have heard of Homer –
>   Or of Dante...[184]

Who wants to be a poet anyway? Isn't that an absolute waste of time?

♪♪

Sharing is an illusion. In this over-shared age, my overriding thought is, why does no one share their money? After all, you only share what is disposably shareable. It's cheap in that sense.

This is something anticipated in a Henry Lawson story, 'Two Sundowners,' in which one says to the other,

'...we've shared and shared alike, and –'
'We never shared money,' said Brummy, decidedly.[185]

True to this day. And all we share are illusions, the illusions of sharing.

Reading Isabel Wilkerson's *Caste: the Lies that Divide Us* brings me to two conclusions: one that the blacks have to gain total independence from the whites in America by creating another democracy in the USA even if it means they'll have to divide the country into two, and the other that Chinese, though often held in world's eyes as the weaker race, are more powerful than their black counterparts, as testified by numerous peasant uprisings in the past that ended up overthrowing the governments, bringing home the truth that the lowest of the low in China can and do at important times of history overthrow the highest of the high.

According to Confucius, what I call the lowest of the low is the earth or 土. To paraphrase him, the earth is where the spring comes out of, the trees grow, along with hundreds of grains, grasses and woods, and birds and animals; it is where life comes out of and death goes into, a place never mindful of its many achievements and that always embraces things.[186]

He's talking about the virtue of modesty, as modest as the earth. But it is what he said about life and death that intrigued me and the connection of the lowest.

Taken out of the context, this is good:

> Every one of us envied the fallen. They were resting under the ground, and in springtime violets would sprout from their bones.[187]

Only last night, In my WeChat communications with a poet in China, I said something to this effect: 'When I die, there's little to be nostalgic about in this world.'

She said, 'Nothing to be nostalgic about.'

Between 1271 and 1295, Marco Polo observes how Chinese women walk; he says,

> The maidens always walk so daintily that they never advance one foot more than a finger's breath beyond the other, since physical integrity is often destroyed by a wanton gait.[188]

He's definitely not aware of the Chinese expression '碎步' (mincing steps), so few people who wrote so much about China having so little knowledge of the Chinese language.

When Mayakovsky says,

> And he who sings not with us today
>   is against
>   us!

he sounds so much like George Bush, who said, 'You are either with us, or with the terrorists.'

But there is so much middle ground, not just either or; being either/or is a kind of terrorism in itself.

White Australia. They wanted the values. But they couldn't do without the cheap labour to do the hard work. See this passage below:

> If White Australia carried the day, and the Kanakas were deported – well, that, to Blanche, was that! That meant the end of the sugar industry. For the sugar industry as she reckoned it, anyhow. Homestead allotments were good enough for these boors, a hundred and odd acres worked by a couple of whites, but for her – no, thank you![189]

The only expression in Chinese that applies to this situation is 又想当婊子，又要立牌坊。

I must admit nothing much I read these days entirely holds my attention. As a result, I generate massive misreadings or extra readings, such as this: 'she had a sudden body,' when I read *Australian Nicknames*. (p. 107)

It's poetry that I created in such moments.

Sir Walter Raleigh. Why 'sir'? Did he submit eventually to the court and all that? Still, I like his poem 'The Lie', particularly these lines that I quote below:

> Say to the court, it glows,
> And shines like rotten wood;
> Say to the church, it shows
> What's good, and doth no good.
> If church and court reply,
> Then give them both the lie.[190]

I think similar things could be said of Australia and its government, too. And another stanza that I like:

> Tell fortune of her blindness;
> Tell nature of decay;
> Tell friendship of unkindness;
> Tell justice of delay.
> And if they will reply,
> Then give them all the lie. (p. 143)

Yeh.

I forgot his name. This is years ago when I watched TV and heard him say that he'd kill anyone in his next story if he or she had got into his bad books. 'A good way of dealing with bad people,' I thought.

I now have another instance of the same, in a letter written by Joseph Roth, in which he says to Pierre Bertaux, among other things,

> He is one of three or four people I would happily murder, with no

more compunction than putting out a cigarette... Sometimes I feel the murderer in me is as natural as the writer, and if I were arrested and put on trial, I would be utterly perplexed.¹⁹¹

For the next few minutes, I'm seriously considering the possibility of starting a murder novel in which I'll have a few people I like the least murdered, including the guy I have never met.

This is something:

...the fact that Hillary Clinton laughed about General Qadaffi's death, after he was torn limb from limb by a mob, the fact that nobody has any manners any more, Hillary, Trump, mobs...¹⁹²

Indeed.

'Transplant' is an important concept in post-colonial culture till you know what it means in the Australian context of nicknames, where it actually refers to someone without a heart. (*See Australian Nicknames*, p. 108)

死间。Death spy. Or Spying by death.

Duke Wu of Zheng, head of the State of Zheng, got his daughter married to the head of the State of Hu. He asked which state was the most appropriate to attack when Guan Qisi, one of his ministers recommended the State of Hu. Furious with the suggestion, he gave the order that Guan be executed. When the head of Hu learnt about the news, he let his guard down against Zheng. As a result, his state was destroyed.¹⁹³

Just learnt this Latin phrase from Sir Thomas Browne – 'Tertullian, *Certum est qua impossibile est*' – and thought how accurate a description this is of my own life.¹⁹⁴

🎵

See this comment on Joseph Brodsky's connection to Tsvetaeva in having one of the techniques to begin a poem, particularly an elegy, on a high note, only to take it to an even higher note:

> 'Novogodnee' [New Year's Greeting: Tsvetaeva's poem on the death of Rilke] begins in typical Tsvetaeva fashion, at the far right – i.e., highest – end of the octave, on high C...with an exclamation directed upward, outward. Throughout the entire poem this tonality, just like the very tenor of this speech, is unvarying: the only possible modification is not a lowering of the register (even in parentheses) but a raising of it. ('Footnote to a Poem', *Less*, 205)[195]

My comment on that is just one word: 'Disgusting!'

Know why? Because, simply put, that's exactly what the poets and all the artists in the Cultural Revolution in China were required to do, to sing the highest praises of Mao Zedong in the highest pitch, and on the highest note, my ears, to this day, filled with the deafening noise of such praises.

Australia, to do it justice, is a pure antidote to that.

🎵

A couple of hours ago, in the middle of translating the book on Brodsky, I saw this:

> In English it is more difficult to lie or, in general, to be ethnically ambiguous.[196]

I noted that by writing these two characters next to it: 放屁!

Then, just now, when I went to the loo and read *The Way of All Flesh* as I pissed into the bowl, I saw this, as if to confirm my suspicion about the lie:

> You are surrounded on every side by lies which would deceive even the elect, if the elect were not generally so uncommonly wide awake... The conscious self of yours, Ernest, is a prig begotten of prigs and trained in priggishness...[197]

Enough said, and in English.

Yesterday (24/6/2021), *Apple Daily* in Hong Kong sold more than 1 million copies and folded. Today, I came across Confucius saying these words in Chinese:

以德以法，夫德法者，御民之具，犹御马之有衔勒也。……
……以万民为马，……故口无声而马应辔，……

Simply put and paraphrased, he's saying that people should be harnessed like horses, with morality and the law, and the silent ones as well.

There you have it, a mirror image of what happened yesterday. But that's China. You can't hope to change them with your short history of two hundred years, one that is much stained with Aboriginal blood, too.

Something that prompted something else in me, quoted,

For the first time in my life I understood why women love their houses and flats more than they love their husbands.[198]

Added to that is their love for their kids, more than anything else, except in one case where the woman left her husband and her daughter for a job in Spain, hardly ever contacting them again. Don't ask me for details; I won't tell.

See. Shortly after that, I read this in Butler's book: 'a woman's love for children'. (*The Way of All Flesh*, p. 129) His description of the aunt's love for her nephew is wonderful stuff. Love it.

Much of China's revolutionary discourse, particularly during the Cultural Revolution, I now understand, must have come under the influence of books like *Journey to the West*, things like 高山低头，河水让路.

Literally translated, it's (letting) the tall mountains lower their heads and the rivers make way for you, slogan-like remarks used to encourage people to make great efforts in their work in transforming Nature.

In *Journey to the West*, a river god causes a miles-wide river to stop flowing to leave the dry ground for the team of the chief monk with his four assistants to walk across it.

If that is a fable, the spirit remains. What the West needs to vanquish is this spirit if they can manage, not the threat, for China, in my opinion, is not a threatful country to anyone but itself.

♪♪

There used to be a tribe in ancient China of the Qiang nationality that has a name that I like: 先零. Literally, First Zero.

I like it. I'll use it as one of my pen-names.

♪♪

The past is a mirror image of the present. Read this passage:

'... It's the so-and-so Chinks they ought to deport and leave the Kanakas alone.'

'... I reckon the Chinese Government would resent its nationals being discriminated against.'

'Who the hell cares about the Chinese Government?'

'The Mother Parliament cares. British Imperialist interests are very much concerned with China, I imagine...'[199]

Now, one only has to make a couple of changes here and there – for example, 'Our Five-eye Ally UK interests' – to make it still valid.

♪♪

Father never went overseas in his life. Yet he learnt English and was widely read in that language. He learnt German in order to be able to read letters written by his second son who was studying in Germany on a government scholarship as a way of helping him along with the language. He learnt Japanese because it was a less corrupt language than English as people were less acquainted with it when he prepared for an examination to qualify as a senior accountant.

He made a remark I remember to this day. 'When it comes to English literature,' he said, 'their novels always end with fights about inheritance and that seems an indication of what the English people are most concerned with.'

When I read the following, that was what I was reminded of:

[Miss Pontifex] wanted someone to leave her money to; she was not going to leave it to people about whom she knew very little, merely because they happened to be sons and daughters of brothers and sisters whom she had never liked. She knew the power and value of money exceedingly well, and how many lovable people suffer and die yearly for the want of it; she was little likely to leave it without being satisfied that her legatees were square, lovable, and more or less hard up…; but if she failed, she must find an heir who was not related to her by blood. (*The Way of All Flesh*, p. 129)

And, by the way, in most Chinese literature, money is not something people talk about, particularly in contemporary literature under the Communist rule.

In his expedition to the Central Shaanxi Plain, Cao Cao (155–220) was able to defeat all his enemies who attacked him together. When his generals asked him what was the secret, Cao Cao said that if his enemies were holding their positions in their own towns or cities, it would be difficult and time-consuming to defeat them one by one. However, when they came together, it's like stringing up all the cocks or roosters together as they lacked coordination and could not work well with each other in a common effort.[200]

A question, on my part, ensued: why did the Eight Powers defeat China in Peking in 1900? Will the new Five Eyes do the same, or be easily overcome as Cao Cao described?

Another girl gone. That's what happened to C. I thought of letters. I thought of how many letters I wrote when I was talking love (谈恋爱) or courting my girlfriend that is my wife. I told him that. I got him to do a keyword search for 'famous love letters' online. He did. Nothing more is heard of what he did letter-wise.

Then I read this:

A lover should pave the way with letters…[201]

Now that we are entering an age of non-verbal communications, why letters, despite the thought that I could still work wonders with letters, given a chance?

Now, how about this:

…jealous of the rich, but incapable of solidarity with the poor.[202]

That's me, I said, to myself.

According to Shakespeare, 'Love sought is good, but given unsought better.' I think I know how that felt.

Read this:

The China I knew had enormous cities with air so polluted people wore oxygen masks with supply tanks just to get through the day. There were cities so polluted, no child born in the last twenty-five years had ever seen a star.
… There was no personal space other than their one tiny room, their one tiny apartment.[203]

Excuse me, I just wanted to say. What are you talking about? It's almost like saying Aboriginal people are still being massacred on a daily basis in Australia.

My main reason for disliking Martin Heidegger with his *Being and Time*[204] is his constant use of Greek words to prove a point or as part of an argument. Unless the world was run in two languages, German and Greek, plus English, this book might be useful. But he has to remember that the sound of 'being' in Chinese is disease (病), or illness, sickness or condition.

When they talk about the threats from China, do they know that the Chinese language at least is not a threat, not to the extent the Greek language is prevalent in Heidegger's book?

Emerson says,

> Society is a joint-stock company, in which the members agree, for the better securing of his bread to each shareholder, to surrender the liberty and culture of the eater. The virtue in most request is conformity. Self-reliance is its aversion. It loves not realities and creators, but names and customs.[205]

The word 'self-reliance' induced a lost memory, historical. Before China was forced to open its gates to the West, it was a self-sufficient and self-reliant country. The English wanted to make money there by selling their opium and other things that China didn't feel a real need for until the former's gunboats pounded on China. Well, the old story.

But the world, the western part of it, is a joint-stock company, in which China is hated because it lacks that 'conformity' and doesn't want to play their game.

According to Solzhenitsyn,

> Stalin and those close to him loved their portraits and splashed them all over the newspapers and issued them in millions of copies.[206]

That's typical Cultural Revolution for you, except that those close to Mao fell fast, like 走马灯.

Robert Menzies says, 'To me, human beings were individuals, and not statistics.' Well, he sounds like an idealist, and a self-deceptive one at that.

But Covid-19 is all about statistics. How many died in the USA, Brazil and India, et cetera, et cetera, all statistics, like in the two world wars, all statistics.

Or perhaps they are individuals when alive and statistics when dead. But even when alive, they are statistics as in demonstrations and protests.

Or we can put it this way: human beings are both individuals and statistics.

While Emerson says, 'Whoso would be a man, must be a nonconformist',[207] the first time I heard this word apply to me in an English-speaking country is when I went to Montreal working as an interpreter for a Chinese hydroelectrical delegation in April 1986. Immediately after we had lunch in Mr Harland's house, one of the delegates sternly suggested we go back to the office and start working while I objected by saying we should follow the local customs. That's when Mr Harland said to me, 'That's fine. Let them do whatever they like. After all, you conform.'

That comment left me a bad aftertaste because I wasn't exactly sure if I should feel delighted with something that actually seemed to sound like a mild criticism.

'…because the girls are better at everything.' (*Ducks, Newburyport*, p. 326)

Oh, yes, I have even gone so far as to consider sex-change, at least that of my characters in my fiction. Who wants to write about a male protagonist any more, particularly an Asian male?

I laughed when I read, 'The expression upon her face he could only describe as "queer"'. (*The Good Soldier*, p. 82)

And a conclusion: the transformation of the words is that of the gender. It would have been much better to invent a completely new word for 'queer' in its contemporary meaning. Instead, an old word, like many other old words, is injected with a new meaning. By comparison, Chinese language is more easily inventable than the English. A most recent coinage: 内卷.

♪♪

Nearly in all classical Chinese fiction, you come across something that you never see in English fiction, or fiction written in English, because it defies translation, any translation. I noticed it but forgot to write about it. It was not till yesterday when I noticed it again, this time in *Journey to the West*, where whenever Sun Wukong, the Monkey King, speaks to the five hundred monks on the beach, he speaks to them in his individual voice. But whenever the five hundred monks speak back, they speak in one voice, represented by this expression: 众僧道.[208]

Literally, that means 'all the monks say'. The more you dwell on this, though, the more you find it impossible for all of them to speak in one voice.

But that is true of *Journey to the West*, of *Water Margin* and of *Dream of the Red Chamber*. Is that an indication of Chinese being no individuals but a faceless mass? I think not. On the contrary, I find it a convenient technique of dealing with the masses, the mob, or the people.

♪♪

You have softly softly. Do you have '默默的道'?[209]

It's a way of saying something in silence or silently-silently saying something.

♪♪

The blurb, by Maria Damon, on the back cover of *Premonitions: the Kaya Anthology of New Asian North American Poetry*, edited by Walter K. Lew, caught my eye with these words: 'Neither a multiculti feel-good anthology…'

My mind was immediately brought back to 1996 when someone from *SMH* interviewed me about Australia. Among other things, I used the words 'pushed back'. That is, living in Australia is a process of being pushed back, with the words constantly said to you: 'No, we are fine with whoever you are as long as you feel comfortable about it yourself.'

Thirty years on, that push-back process is complete, with the help of 'multiculti' Australia. One feels one lives in a foreign country that will always hold one as an outcast, a foreigner, an outsider because the place has achieved the success of excluding one for good.

♪♪♪

When Joseph Roth wrote in a letter that 'I get by on 5 marks a day' (*A Life in Letters*, p. 160), I thought of Wu, a roommate I had in the early days of 1991 and 1992 when we shared accommodation with each other and a number of other students doing PhD at La Trobe U. On one occasion, he excitedly reported to me that he had cut down his weekly expenses to five Australian dollars, going to the market at the conclusion of it when everything was sold for cheap with the crying of 'two dollars', 'one dollar' and 'fifty cents' the lot, and where he bought self-raising flour to make steamed bread instead of buying bread, and all those strategies of less buying or non-buying because, I remember, he even had his electrical switches and plugs shipped from China, too.

♪♪♪

I'm tired of having an agent who keeps telling me to adapt my finished manuscript for the various needs of the publishers. If she or he wants to do that again, I shall quote Joseph Roth as saying, about his finished novel, sent to Stefan Zweig for reviewing,

> I for my part find it superfluous to have written it. I have no ties to it any more. I'm tired of it, or I am simply tired. I don't think the book can engage me any more than I can engage myself. Believe me, I've been a burden to myself for years. (*A Life in Letters*, p. 161)

Indeed, I often feel like digging up a corpse from the ground and embellishing it for the money. After all, Alex, my writer friend, often tells me that when he finishes a novel it feels more like giving death to a book than giving birth.

♪♪♪

More than seven hundred years ago, Marco Polo notices that the Chinese don't like wine but prefer their own rice-based wine. He says,

Grapes and wine are not produced locally; but raisins of excellent quality are imported from other ports and so too is wine, though the inhabitants do not set much store by this, being accustomed to the wine made of rice and spices.[210]

Things in China today have been almost completely reversed in a situation where most people prefer foreign-imported wine to display their wealth and to show off, both a boon and bane to Australia, depending on the bilateral relationship of the two countries.

We lived through it; we forgot it. I meant I. I meant the Cultural Revolution (1966–1976) until I read the book and I remembered.

This is what Mao said about the intellectuals. According to him, the lowest people are the most intelligent while the highest people are the most stupid.

And in the article I read, the writer said that in those days 'the intellectuals had brains filled with the rubbish of capitalist individualism, liberalism and anarchism'.[211]

I was one of such intellectuals myself, wasn't I?

I never believe in muses. But what Ovid says here has my agreement when he says that poets are,

> ...the Muses' darlings, contain
> A divine spark. God is in us, we have dealings with heaven...[212]

I was tempted to keep 'Dealings with Heaven' as a future title. We'll see.

Something similar or parallel to what happened under Mao. According to Solzhenitsyn, in the USSR, those who got purged were

> too independent, too influential, along with those who were too well-to-do, too intelligent, too noteworthy.' (*The Gulag Archipelago*, p. 77)

I am a bit tired of that, in China or in the Soviet Union. I wonder if it is the human trait, something so evil within the human nature, that ignorance will reign supreme everywhere in different historical times, in America with its caste system and in Australia with its unchanged racist nature.

The remark 'comparisons are odious', or 'odorous' in Shakespeare's *Much Ado About Nothing* serves always as a reminder of my own mother's words: 人比人，气死人. Literally, people compare people, anger people dead.

Paraphrased and longer-winded, it means when you compare people with people, or compare yourself with other people, you will die in anger, or you'll be angered to death.

Mark Twain begins his 'Advice to Youth' with this remark, 'Always obey your parents',[213] that made him sound like a Confucian-educated Chinese.

See what Confucius says about one's respect to one's parents:

生，事之以礼；死，葬之以礼，祭之以礼。

Treat your parents with respect when they are alive and bury them with respect when they die.

Since I mention Confucius, I might mention more of him, particularly what he said here:

知可为，知不可为；知可言，知不可言；知可行，知不可行。

A direct translation would render this as

Know the doable and the undoable; know the sayable and the unsayable; know the practicable and the impracticable.

For a writer, though, this could be altered to become: know the writeable and the unwritable. And it applies to both China and Australia, the former in which nothing much is writeable, for political reasons, and the latter in which nothing much is writeable, either, because of censorship for both economic and political reasons.

♪♪♪

This, nothing extraordinary, is nevertheless true:

> I have come to be very much of a cynic in these matters; I mean that it is impossible to believe in the permanence of man's or woman's love. Or, at any rate, it is impossible to believe in the permanence of any early passion. As I see it, at least, with regard to man, a love affair, a love for any definite woman, is something in the nature of a widening of the experience. (*The Good Soldier*, p. 82)

As far as I know, it's also a widening of the experience for women, too, in this day and age, when it is often the women who take the initiative in such matters. And love is as impermanent as the running water of a creek or a river; it stays here one moment and is gone the next although that moment, to some, lasts forever.

♪♪♪

When I read 'none can know each other but those who have played together as children' (*The Way of All Flesh*, p. 141) I thought how true that is.

After my childhood spent in Huangzhou, Hubei, China, few, if any, can ever know me or I them. I had to laugh out loud at how erroneous some of the academic papers or theses got me wrong in their discussions of my books.

Go back to my childhood, meet with my childhood mates, or else don't even bother about my books, I said to them in my imagination.

♪♪♪

Solitude is my life, even in a crowd, even in the sexual couplings, part of the reason why I like Emerson's words when he says,

> ...but the great man is he who in the midst of the crowd keeps with perfect sweetness with the independence of solitude.[214]

♪♪

I was going into the kitchen to refill my mug with more hot water when she drew my attention to what she was doing: preparing to make dumplings with minced beef while commenting that this was what my auntie liked.

For a moment, I was caught off guard before I realised who she was referring to. It's the wife of my Big Uncle, my own mother's eldest brother. Then, memory rushed back as I said, 'In the poor old days, they were lucky because she was of the Hui nationality and as she was entitled to beef rationing whereas people of the Han origin had no such luck.'

Another memory followed as I sat back before my computer and wrote the above. In Big Uncle's place, whenever I was there, they treated me to the beef. But because I didn't like it, Big Uncle had to lie about it, saying it was horsemeat. As a result, I was duped to eat it.

♪♪

I came across another reference to white faces in ancient Chinese fiction. When he crosses the boundary line with his two disciples, Tang Sangzang, a reincarnation of the famous Buddhist monk, Xuanzang, once again falls into the hands of a monster in Journey to the West, and is described by a local elderly person as a '白脸的胖和尚', fat monk with a white face.[215]

A host of references follow from there, reminding me once again that white faces in Chinese culture are often associated with justice, beauty and righteousness.

♪♪

English language is one prone to mistakes, very much resembling its Chinese counterpart. Every time I key in characters, I almost always get the wrong ones before I correct them, for example, 北京 for 背景, 墓地 for 目的, 轻浮 for 情妇, et cetera.

I recalled all that when I read, 'You stop my toung, and teach my hart to speake…'[216] Three mistakes in one short line!

Unlike its English counterpart, much of the written Chinese remains unbrokenly the same for millennia.

A line, 'taste of my cock still fresh in your mouth…'[217]

Well, I would have added a line to that that goes, 'and on your toung, I tasted the taste of my own cock.'

He names names in his last book: Malraux, Mauriac, Maurois, Michaux, Michima, Montherland and Morand.

Then, at the end of another sentence, he says, 'all those writers were stunning mediocrities'.[218] How lovely is that!

Two things he says in that book that I don't find particularly interesting because of no story but persist in reading, for years, from 5 March 2014, are as follows, one that goes,

> I guess it is vanity that makes most of us keep straight, if we do keep straight, in this world.[219]

My response to that: yes, like poetry.
And the other that goes,

> For it is intolerable to live constantly with one human being who perceives one's small meannesses. It is really death to do so – that is why so many marriages turn out unhappily.[220]

And my response to that is twofold, that it takes two, not just one, to pick on and find fault with each other, and that it's the same with living in a country for too long as all its meannesses will disgust one to the degree of fatigue. Hence migration, spiritual if not physical.

Zhao Rui, mentioned before, says in his book that

亡者非丧其身，谓沉之于渊。沉之于渊者，谓夺其威，废其权。[221]

Paraphrased, it means you don't physically destroy your ministers who have won battles. But you reduce their position and power to the bottom, an extension of the saying, 高鸟尽，良弓藏。

But, perversely, the reduction to the bottom remark painfully reminds me of intellectuals lying in waste in a country like Australia simply because they are deemed an integral non-part of the country except as economic wastrels.

It is interesting to know that Li Bai was a close friend of Zhao Rui's, a strategist in his own right who chose to live a hermit's life and, on numerous occasions, knocked back Emperor Xuanzong of Tang's invitation to be a court advisor.

Notes

1. 'Tempest,' *The Complete Works of William Shakespeare.* Atlantis, 1980, p. 11.
2. Tsevetaeva, quoted in David M. Bethea, *Joseph Brodsky and the Creation of Exile.* Princeton University Press, 1994, p. 180.
3. E.M. Cioran, *The Trouble with Being Born.* The Arcade Publishing, 2012 [1973], p. 176.
4. Evelyn Conlon, *Skin of Dreams.* Brandon/Mount Eagle Publications, 2003, p. 100.
5. E.M. Cioran, *The Trouble with Being Born.* The Arcade Publishing, 2012 [1973], p. 187.
6. Michael Hofmann (trans./ed.). Granta Books, 2013, p. 39.
7. E.M. Cioran, *Drawn and Quartered.* Skyhorse Publishing, 2012 [1971], p. 37.
8. David Day, Claiming a Continent: A New History of Australia. HarperPerennial, 2005 [1996], pp. 267–8.
9. E.M. Cioran, *Drawn and Quartered.* Skyhorse Publishing, 2012 [1971], p. 38.
10. E.M. Cioran, *History and Utopia.* The Arcade Publishing, 2015 [1960], p. 116.
11. Ibid., p. 117.
12. Trans. John Macquarrie and Edward Robinson. Harper & Row, 1962, p. 22.
13. Trans. Michael Hofmann. Granta Publications, 2013 [1938], p. 1.
14. Quoted in Robert Menzies, *Afternoon Light: Some Memories of Men and Events.* Penguin, 1970 [1967]. p. 6. Sampson was Menzies' grandfather.
15. See 钱春绮,《歌德名诗精选》。太白文艺出版社, 1997, 第129页。
16. See his *The Collected Poems of Kenneth Koch.* Alfred A. Knopf, 2019, p. 468.
17. Marlo Morgan, *Mutant Message Down Under.* HarperCollins, 1994 [1991], p. 68.
18. E.M. Cioran, *The Trouble with Being Born.* The Arcade Publishing, 2012 [1973], p. 191.
19. Quoted in Lily Xiao Hong Lee, *The Virtue of Yin: Studies on Chinese Women.* Wild Peony, 1994, p. 91.
20. Ibid., p. 92.
21. Quoted in *Ralph Waldo Emerson, Selected Essays, Lectures, and Poems,* ed. Robert D. Richardson

Jr. Bantam Classic, 2007 [1990], p. 5.
22. E.M. Cioran, *The Trouble with Being Born*. The Arcade Publishing, 2012 [1973], p. 192.
23. E.M. Cioran, *The Trouble with Being Born*. The Arcade Publishing, 2012 [1973], p. 192.
24. See Luo Guanzhong et al, *Sanguo yanyi* (Romance of the Three Kingdoms). China Youth Publishing House, 1992, p. 652.
25. Ibid., p. 676.
26. E.M. Cioran, *The Trouble with Being Born*. The Arcade Publishing, 2012 [1973], p. 193.
27. E.M. Cioran, *Drawn and Quartered*. Skyhorse Publishing, 2012 [1971], p. 64.
28. Quoted in Lily Xiao Hong Lee, *The Virtue of Yin: Studies on Chinese Women*. Wild Peony, 1994, p. 93.
29. E.M. Cioran, *Drawn and Quartered*. Skyhorse Publishing, 2012 [1971], p. 37.
30. This is *Oscar & Lucinda* by Peter Carey that I bought second-hand.
31. Quoted in 丁永淮（等）编注《苏东坡黄州作品全编》。武汉出版社, 1996 年, p. 202.
32. Quoted in *Ralph Waldo Emerson, Selected Essays, Lectures, and Poems*, ed. Robert D. Richardson Jr. Bantam Classic, 2007 [1990], p. 7.
33. Ibid., p. 7.
34. See *Being and Time*, trans. John Macquarrie and Edward Robinson. Harper & Row, in 1962, p. 23.
35. Routledge & Kegan Paul, 1960 [1950], p. 47.
36. Quoted in 丁永淮（等）编注《苏东坡黄州作品全编》。武汉出版社, 1996 年, p. 211.
37. E.M. Cioran, *The Trouble with Being Born*. The Arcade Publishing, 2012 [1973], p. 202.
38. Quoted in 丁永淮（等）编注《苏东坡黄州作品全编》。武汉出版社, 1996 年, p. 213.
39. E.M. Cioran, *The Trouble with Being Born*. The Arcade Publishing, 2012 [1973], pp. 199–203.
40. Joseph Roth, *A Life in Letters*, trans./ed. Michael Hofmann. Granta Books, 2013, p. 49.
41. Samuel Butler, *The Way of All Flesh*. Penguin, 1953 [1903], p. 62.
42. *The Norton Anthology of Poetry*, fourth edition. W.W. Norton, 1996 [1970], p. 63.
43. Quoted in 丁永淮（等）编注《苏东坡黄州作品全编》。武汉出版社, 1996 年, p. 202.
44. David Day, *Claiming a Continent: A New History of Australia*. HarperPerennial, 2005 [1996], pp. 285.
45. E.M. Cioran, *The Trouble with Being Born*. The Arcade Publishing, 2012 [1973], p. 176.
46. Harold Pinter, *The Dwarfs*. Faber & Faber, 1990, p. 57.
47. Lucy Ellmann, *Ducks, Newburyport*. Galley Beggar Press, 2019, p. 291.
48. Martin Heidegger, *Being and Time*, trans. John Macquarrie and

Edward Robinson. Harper & Row, 1962, p. 26.
49. E.M. Cioran, *The Trouble with Being Born*. The Arcade Publishing, 2012 [1973], p. 206.
50. E.M. Cioran, *Drawn and Quartered*. Skyhorse Publishing, 2012 [1971], p. 73.
51. Quoted from https://en.wikipedia.org/wiki/Helen_Quach
52. Samuel Butler, *The Way of All Flesh*. Penguin, 1953 [1903], p. 64.
53. Taffy Davies, *Australian Nicknames*. Rigby, 1977, p. 39.
54. Henry Handel Richardson, *The Getting of Wisdom*. Heinemann Educational Books, 1978 [1910], p. 184.
55. E.M. Cioran, *The Trouble with Being Born*. The Arcade Publishing, 2012 [1973], p. 209.
56. *The Norton Anthology of Poetry*, fourth edition. W.W. Norton, 1996 [1970], p. 63.
57. Joseph Roth, *A Life in Letters*, trans./ed. Michael Hofmann, Granta Books, 2013, p. 49.
58. See this remark: 'lead an honest and clean life; refuse to be contaminated by evil influence', quoted here: https://baike.baidu.com/item/洁身自好
59. A found poem from Patrick White, *The Living and the Dead*. Eyre & Spottiswoode, 1962 [1941], p. 241.
60. Marlo Morgan, *Mutant Message Down Under*. HarperCollins, 1994 [1991], pp. 63–4.
61. Taffy Davies, *Australian Nicknames*. Rigby, 1977, p. 43.
62. See *The Collected Poems of Kenneth Koch*. Alfred A. Knopf, 2019, p. 491.
63. Quoted in 丁永淮(等)编注《苏东坡黄州作品全编》。武汉出版社, 1996 年, p.252 and translated by Ouyang.
64 Quoted from his *The Collected Poems of Kenneth Koch*. Alfred A. Knopf, 2019, p. 503.
65. Quoted in *Ralph Waldo Emerson, Selected Essays, Lectures, and Poems*, ed. Robert D. Richardson Jr. Bantam Classic, 2007 [1990], p. 21.
66. Henry Lawson, *Send Round the Hat*. Angus & Robertson, 1924, p. 19.
67. Patrick White, *The Living and the Dead*. Eyre & Spottiswoode, 1962 [1941], p. 275.
68. Quoted in *Ralph Waldo Emerson, Selected Essays, Lectures, and Poems*, ed. Robert D. Richardson Jr. Bantam Classic, 2007 [1990], p. 25.
69. 'Listening to the river' by Su Shi, in *Best of Both Words: Classical Chinese Poetry in English Translation*, trans. Ouyang Yu. ASM, 2012, p. 55.
70. Henry Lawson, *Send Round the Hat*. Angus & Robertson, 1924.
71. E.M. Cioran, *Drawn and Quartered*. Skyhorse Publishing, 2012 [1971], p. 95.
72. Ovid, *The Erotic Poems*. Penguin, 1982, p. 183.

73. 'Aesthetics of stone', *The Collected Poems of Kenneth Koch*. Alfred A. Knopf, 2019, p. 510.
74. Joseph Roth, *A Life in Letters*, trans./ed. Michael Hofmann, Granta Books, 2013, p. 66.
75. Ovid, *The Erotic Poems*. Penguin, 1982, p. 185.
76. Heinemann Educational Books 1978 [1910], p. 196.
77. Folio Society, 1997 [1958], p. 134.
78. Robert Menzies, *Afternoon Light: Some Memories of Men and Events*. Penguin, 1970 [1967]. p. 27.
79. Jean Devanny, *Cindie*. Virago, 1986 [1949], p. 46.
80. Kenneth Koch, *The Collected Poems of Kenneth Koch*. Alfred A. Knopf, 2019, p. 516.
81. Robert Frost, quoted in John Updike, *Due Considerations*, 2007, p. 535.
82. Henry Handel Richardson, *The Getting of Wisdom*. Heinemann Educational Books, 1978 [1910], p. 199.
83. Craig McGregor, *Don't Talk To Me About Love*. Penguin, 1972.
84. Ralph Waldo Emerson, *Selected Essays, Lectures, and Poems*, ed. Robert D. Richardson Jr. Bantam Classic, 2007 [1990], p. 28.
85. Quoted in the Introduction, Wordsworth Editions, 2002 [1995], p. XI.
86. Patrick White, quoted in David Day, *Claiming a Continent: A New History of Australia*. HarperPerennial, 2005 [1996], p. 339.
87. Written by Ouyang Yu.
88. Evelyn Conlon, *Skin of Dreams*. Brandon/Mount Eagle Publications, 2003, p. 194.
89. Marlo Morgan, *Mutant Message Down Under*. HarperCollins, 1994 [1991], p. 165.
90. Harold Pinter, *The Dwarfs*. Faber & Faber, 1990, p. 57.
91. Alma Classics, 2013 [1915].
92. *The Travels of Marco Polo*. Translated and introduced by Ronald Latham. Folio Society, 1997 [1958], p. 134.
93. Samuel Butler, *The Way of All Flesh*. Penguin, 1953 [1903], p. 62.
94. Ovid, *The Erotic Poems*. Penguin, 1982, p. 189.
95. *The Norton Anthology of Poetry*, fourth edition. W.W. Norton, 1996 [1970], p. 108.
96. All translations in English mine unless otherwise noted.
97. Quoted in Ouyang Yu, 《随译集》(*Translations Randomly Rendered*). Otherland Publishing, 2021, p. 286.
98. Ibid., p. 287.
99. David Day, *Claiming a Continent: A New History of Australia*. HarperPerennial, 2005 [1996], p. 357.
100. Quoted in ibid., p. 357.
101. Name of a character, whose real name is Ella Marchmill, also a character in 'An Imaginative Woman', in Thomas Hardy's *Life's Little Ironies*. Wordsworth Editions, 1995, p. 5.
102. Thomas Hardy, 'An Imaginative

Woman', *Life's Little Ironies*. Wordsworth Editions, 1995, p. 5.
103. Evelyn Conlon, *Skin of Dreams*. Brandon/Mount Eagle Publications, 2003, p. 204.
104. Harold Pinter, *The Dwarfs*. Faber & Faber, 1990, p. 87.
105. Patrick White, *The Living and the Dead*. Eyre & Spottiswoode, 1962 [1941], p. 284.
106. Ibid., p. 285.
107. Craig McGregor, *Don't Talk To Me About Love*. Penguin, 1972, p. 79.
108. Sax Rohmer, *The Hand of Fu Manchu, The Return of D Fu Manchu, The Yellow Claw, Dope: 4 Complete Classics*. Castle, 1983, p. 4.
109. 赵蕤，《长短经》（下）。中州古籍出版社，2007, p. 380.
110. Evelyn Conlon, *Skin of Dreams*. Brandon/Mount Eagle Publications, 2003, p. 209.
111. Quoted in 丁永淮（等）编注《苏东坡黄州作品全编》。武汉出版社，1996 年, p. 364.
112. Quoted in ibid., p. 371.
113. Ibid., p. 371.
114. Taffy Davies, Australian Nicknames. Rigby Ltd, 1977, p. 61.
115. Ovid, *The Erotic Poems*. Penguin , 1982, p. 194.
116. E.M. Cioran, *Drawn and Quartered*. Skyhorse Publishing, 2012 [1971], p. 109.
117. Sax Rohmer, *The Hand of Fu Manchu, The Return of Dr. Fu Manchu, The Yellow Claw, Dope: 4 Complete Classics*. Castle, 1983, p. 5.
118. Evelyn Conlon, *Skin of Dreams*. Brandon/Mount Eagle Publications, 2003, p. 231.
119. Harold Pinter, *The Dwarfs*. Faber & Faber, 1990, p. 93.
120 Henry Lawson, Send Round the Hat. Angus & Robertson, 1924, p. 51.
121. Taffy Davies, *Australian Nicknames*. Rigby, 1977, p. 43.
122. Mikhail Sholokhov, *The Don Flows Home to the Sea*. Penguin, 1976 [1940], p. 44.
123. 范文澜（著），《中国通史简编》（修订本第三编第二册）。人民出版社出版: 1965 [1955], p. 556.
124. *The Norton Anthology of Poetry*, fourth edition. W.W. Norton, 1996 [1970], p. 111A .
125. Isabel Wilkerson, *Caste: the Lies that Divide Us*. Allen Lane, 2020, p. xv.
126. Ouyang Yu, 'Domestic politics', *Westerly*, no. 2, winter, 1997, pp. 26–7.
127. 赵蕤，《长短经》（下）。中州古籍出版社，2007, p. 411.
128. Alexander Solzhenitshyn, *The Gulag Archipelago*. Collins/Harvill Press, 1974, p. 32.
129. Quoted in Abdelwahab Meddeb's poem 'I Take the Path', in which he says, 'I take the path, that leads to the garden of error, I play with names, behind the grove of truth.' See *The Yale Anthology of Twentieth-Century French Poetry*,

ed. Mary Ann Caws. Yale University Press, 2004, p. 419.
130. Quoted in 丁永淮(等)编注《苏东坡黄州作品全编》。武汉出版社, 1996 年, p. 445.
131. 赵蕤,《长短经》(下)。中州古籍出版社, 2007, pp. 414–5.
132. Quoted in 丁永淮(等)编注《苏东坡黄州作品全编》。武汉出版社. 1996 年, p. 453.
133. 曹雪芹、高鹗(著),《红楼梦》。黄山书社, 1983, p. 218.
134. 吴承恩,《西游记》(新批本)。江苏古籍出版社, 1992, p. 224.
135. *The Norton Anthology of Poetry*, fourth edition. W.W. Norton, 1996 [1970], p. 117.
136. Ouyang Yu, *Moon over Melbourne and Other Poems*. Papyrus Publishing, 1995, p. 8.
137. Isabel Wilkerson, *Caste: the Lies that Divide Us*. Allen Lane, 2020, p. 7.
138. Thomas Hardy, 'An Imaginative Woman', *Life's Little Ironies*. Wordsworth Editions, 1995, p. 54.
139. Quoted in 丁永淮(等)编注《苏东坡黄州作品全编》。武汉出版社, 1996 年, p. 535.
140. David M. Bethea, *Joseph Brodsky and the Creation of Exile*. Princeton University Press, 1994, pp. 5–6.
141. Ibid., p. 9.
142. Robert Menzies, *Afternoon Light: Some Memories of Men and Events*. Penguin, 1970 [1967]. p. 53.
143. Quoted in 丁永淮(等)编注《苏东坡黄州作品全编》。武汉出版社, 1996 年, p. 577.
144. Quoted in David M. Bethea, *Joseph Brodsky and the Creation of Exile*. Princeton University Press, 1994, p. 13.
145. Sax Rohmer, *The Hand of Fu Manchu, The Return of Dr. Fu Manchu, The Yellow Claw, Dope: 4 Complete Classics*. Castle, 1983.
146. Alexander Solzhenitshyn, *The Gulag Archipelago*. Collins/Harvill Press, 1974, p. 37.
147. Kenneth Koch, *The Collected Poems of Kenneth Koch*. Alfred A. Knopf, 2019, p. 541.
148. Ouyang Yu, *Moon over Melbourne and Other Poems*. Papyrus Publishing, 1995, p. 46.
149. David M. Bethea, *Joseph Brodsky and the Creation of Exile*. Princeton University Press, 1994, pp. 24–5.
150. Joseph Roth, *A Life in Letters*, trans./ed. Michael Hofmann, Granta Books, 2013, p. 130.
151. Craig McGregor, *Don't Talk To Me About Love*. Penguin, 1972, p. 112.
152. Henry Howard, Earl of Surrey, 'The Soote Season', *The Norton Anthology of Poetry*, fourth edition. W.W. Norton, 1996 [1970], p. 123.
153. Joseph Roth, *A Life in Letters*, trans./ed. Michael Hofmann, Granta Books, 2013, p. 118.
154. Mikhail Sholokhov, *The Don Flows Home to the Sea*. Penguin Books, 1976 [1940], p. 57.

155. 吴承恩，《西游记》(新批本)。江苏古籍出版社, 1992, pp. 273–4.
156. Heather Rose, *Bruny*. Allen & Unwin, 2019, p. 26.
157. Thomas Hardy, 'To Please His Wife', *Life's Little Ironies*. Wordsworth Editions, 1995, p. 98.
158. *Ralph Waldo Emerson, Selected Essays, Lectures, and Poems*, ed. Robert D. Richardson Jr. Bantam Classic, 2007 [1990], p. 46.
159. Samuel Butler, *The Way of All Flesh*. Penguin, 1953 [1903], p. 98.
160. Quoted in *Ralph Waldo Emerson, Selected Essays, Lectures, and Poems*, ed. Robert D. Richardson Jr. Bantam Classic, 2007 [1990], pp. 51–2.
161. Quoted in Robert Menzies, *Afternoon Light: Some Memories of Men and Events*. Penguin Boks, 1970 [1967], p. 6. Sampson was Menzies' grandfather.
162. Ouyang Yu, *Moon over Melbourne and Other Poems*. Papyrus Publishing, 1995, p. 21.
163. Samuel Butler, *The Way of All Flesh*. Penguin, 1953 [1903], pp. 102–3.
164. Craig McGregor, *Don't Talk To Me About Love*. Penguin , 1972, p. 127.
165. *The Norton Anthology of Poetry*, fourth edition. W.W. Norton, 1996 [1970], p. 135.
166. Samuel Butler, *The Way of All Flesh*. Penguin, 1953 [1903], p. 104.
167. Taffy Davies, *Australian Nicknames*. Rigby, 1977, p. 102.
168. Isabel Wilkerson, *Caste, The Lies That Divide Us*. Allen Lane: 2020, pp. 52–3.
169. See it here: https://www.liminalmag.com/interviews/ouyang-yu
170. Quoted in David M. Bethea, *Joseph Brodsky and the Creation of Exile*. Princeton University Press, 1994, p. 59.
171. Joseph Roth, *A Life in Letters*, trans./ed. Michael Hofmann, Granta Books, 2013, p. 130.
172. Ibid.
173. Robert Menzies, *Afternoon Light: Some Memories of Men and Events*. Penguin, 1970 [1967]. p. 108.
174. *Ralph Waldo Emerson, Selected Essays, Lectures, and Poems*, ed. Robert D. Richardson Jr. Bantam Classic, 2007 [1990], p. 112.
175. Jean Devanny, *Cindie*. Virago, 1986 [1949], p. 77.
176. Alexander Solzhenitshyn, *The Gulag Archipelago*. Collins/Harvill Press, 1974, p. 32.
177. 赵蕤，《长短经》(下)。中州古籍出版社, 2007, p. 470.
178. Quoted in Isabel Wilkerson, *Caste: the Lies that Divide Us*. Allen Lane, 2020, p. 79.
179. Taffy Davies, *Australian Nicknames*. Rigby, 1977, p. 102.
180. 刘小萌等，《中国知青事典》。四川人民出版社, 1995.
181. Samuel Butler, *The Way of All Flesh*. Penguin, 1953 [1903], p. 62.
182. Ford Madox Ford, *The Good Soldier*. Alma Classics, 2013 [1915], p. 81.

183. Ovid, *The Erotic Poems*. Penguin, 1982, p. 226.
184. Ibid.
185. Henry Lawson, *Send Round the Hat*. Angus & Robertson, 1924, p. 109.
186. His original Chinese words are here: https://zhidao.baidu.com/question/380842702.html
187. Joseph Roth, *A Life in Letters*, trans./ed. Michael Hofmann, Granta Books, 2013, p. 136.
188. *The Travels of Marco Polo*. Translated and introduced by Ronald Latham. Folio Society, 1997 [1958], p. 166.
189. Jean Devanny, *Cindie*. Virago, 1986 [1949], p. 80.
190. *The Norton Anthology of Poetry*, fourth edition. W.W. Norton, 1996 [1970], p. 142.
191. Joseph Roth, *A Life in Letters*, trans./ed. Michael Hofmann, Granta Books, 2013, p. 49.
192. Lucy Ellmann, *Ducks, Newburyport*. Galley Beggar Press Ltd, 2019, pp. 325–326.
193. 赵蕤, 《长短经》（下）。中州古籍出版社, 2007, p. 474.
194. See it quoted here: https://penelope.uchicago.edu/relmed/relmed.html
195. Quoted in David M. Bethea, *Joseph Brodsky and the Creation of Exile*. Princeton University Press, 1994, p. 95.
196. Ibid., p. 121.
197. Samuel Butler, *The Way of All Flesh*. Penguin, 1953 [1903], p. 123.
198. Joseph Roth, *A Life in Letters*, trans./ed. Michael Hofmann, Granta Books, 2013, p. 159.
199. Jean Devanny, *Cindie*. Virago, 1986 [1949], pp. 138-9.
200. See 赵蕤, 《长短经》（下）。中州古籍出版社, 2007, p. 492.
201. Ovid, *The Erotic Poems*. Penguin, 1982, p. 228.
202. Joseph Roth, *A Life in Letters*, trans./ed. Michael Hofmann, Granta Books, 2013, p. 151.
203. Heather Rose, *Bruny*. Allen & Unwin, 2019, pp. 190–1.
204. See Martin Heidegger, *Being and Time*, trans. John Macquarrie and Edward Robinson. Harper & Row, 1962, p. 56.
205. *Ralph Waldo Emerson, Selected Essays, Lectures, and Poems*, ed. Robert D. Richardson Jr. Bantam Classic, 2007 [1990], p. 153.
206. Alexander Solzhenitshyn, *The Gulag Archipelago*. Collins/Harvill Press, 1974, p. 75.
207. *Ralph Waldo Emerson, Selected Essays, Lectures, and Poems*, ed. Robert D. Richardson Jr. Bantam Classic, 2007 [1990], p. 153.
208. 吴承恩, 《西游记》（新批本）。江苏古籍出版社, 1992, p. 513.
209. Ibid., p. 523.
210. *The Travels of Marco Polo*. Translated and introduced by Ronald Latham. Folio Society, 1997 [1958], p. 181.
211. 刘小萌等, 《中国知青事典》。四川人民出版社, 1995, p. 138.
212. Ovid, *The Erotic Poems*. Penguin, 1982, p. 230.

213. Quoted in Quentin Miller, *The Generation of Ideas: A Thematic Reader.* Peking University Press, 2006, p. 33.
214. *Ralph Waldo Emerson, Selected Essays, Lectures, and Poems*, ed. by Robert D. Richardson Jr. Bantam Classic, 2007 [1990], p. 155.
215. 吴承恩，《西游记》（新批本）。江苏古籍出版社, 1992, p. 588.
216. Quoted in Edmund Spenser, 'Amoretti', in *The Norton Anthology of Poetry*, fourth edition. W.W. Norton, 1996 [1970], p. 166.
217. Timothy Liu, 'With Chaos in Each Kiss', *Premonitions: the Kaya Anthology of New Asian North American Poetry*, ed. Walter K. Lew. Kaya Production, 1995, p. 333.
218. Vladimir Nabokov, *The Original of Laura*. Alfred A. Knopf, 2008, p. 95.
219. Ford Madox Ford, *The Good Soldier*. Alma Classics, 2013 [1915], p. 86.
220. Ibid., p. 86.
221. 赵蕤,《长短经》（下）。中州古籍出版社, 2007, p. 518.

www.ingramcontent.com/pod-product-compliance
Lightning Source LLC
Chambersburg PA
CBHW021105080526
44587CB00010B/387